Historical Perspectives on Business
Enterprise Series

Werner von Siemens

Inventor and International Entrepreneur

Wilfried Feldenkirchen

Ohio State University Press
Columbus

Originally published as
Werner von Siemens: Erfinder und internationaler Unternehmer,
© 1992 Siemens Aktiengesellschaft

Library of Congress Cataloging-in-Publication Data

Feldenkirchen, Wilfried.
[Werner von Siemens. English]
Werner von Siemens : inventor and international entrepreneur /
Wilfried Feldenkirchen.
p. cm. — (Historical perspectives on business enterprise series)
Includes bibliographical references.
ISBN 0–8142–0658–1. — ISBN 0–8142–0659–X (pbk.)
1. Siemens, Werner von, 1816–1892. 2. Electric engineers—Germany—
Biography. 3. Businessmen—Germany—Biography.
4. Electric engineering—Germany—History—19th century.
5. Business enterprises—Germany—History—19th century.
I. Title. II. Series.
TK140 .S5F4513   1994
338.7'6213'092—dc20
[B]   94–29670
CIP

Text design by John Delaine.
Type set in Sabon with Optima display.
Printed by Edwards Brothers, Ann Arbor, MI.

The paper in this book meets the guidelines for permanence and durability of the
Committee on Production Guidelines for Book Longevity of the Council on
Library Resources.

9   8   7   6   5   4   3   2   1

Contents

Editors' Preface

The publication of this book marks an important milestone for our series, Historical Perspectives on Business Enterprise. Historians have long engaged in biographical scholarship and writing, knowing that ultimately it is the actions of individuals that make history. Business historians have been especially fascinated with the stories of entrepreneurship and individuals, knowing that successful business activity requires leadership and individual action as well as teamwork and organization.

It is particularly significant that we offer this study of Werner von Siemens, written by one of Germany's most able business historians, in English translation. Siemens's name is a household word in Germany, where he is studied in school as a figure prominent in that nation's nineteenth-century industrial growth and thus in its rise to nationhood. In Germany the firm that bears Siemens's name is also well known as a supplier of electrical and electronic goods of all kinds. However, Siemens the man and Siemens the company are less well known in the English-speaking world than their importance merits. The publication of this biography is thus an important contribution to our historical knowledge, bringing to light a major entrepreneurial life and, especially, explaining the integration of technological invention and business acumen in the career of Werner von Siemens.

Siemens is best known in the English-speaking world as a pioneering inventor and electrical engineer. Shortly after World War II, Werner's descendant Georg Siemens wrote a two-volume study, *History of the House of Siemens,* published in English in 1957 (Freiburg: Karl Alber; reprinted, New York:

Arno Press, 1977). Georg Siemens's study was an examination of the institution, "the House" of Siemens, a combination of businesses that emanated from the initiatives of Werner von Siemens. The *History of the House of Siemens* focused mainly on the technological developments associated with Siemens and the business that carried his name. It told an important story in the history of technology, for Siemens was associated with all sorts of innovations in telegraphy and in electrical generation, transmission, and application. After the founder's death, the company continued to expand its range of electrical technologies, not the least of which was telephony.

Wilfried Feldenkirchen's biography of Werner von Siemens, however, goes well beyond the story of invention. Feldenkirchen has used archival records unavailable in the 1940s to tell a story of the combination of kinship, entrepreneurship, and invention. What emerges is an explanation of a business figure whose importance is on a par with, say, that of Andrew Carnegie or John D. Rockefeller, to name two of Siemens's best known contemporaries in America. Although, unlike Carnegie and Rockefeller, Siemens did not especially advance the science of business management and organization, in contrast to them, he was technically brilliant and combined his engineering brilliance with the development of a business whose activities at an early stage nearly spanned the globe. Like Carnegie and Rockefeller, Siemens established a firm that persisted and expanded after the founder left its active management.

The differences between those nineteenth-century giants of industrial enterprise stemmed in part from dissimilarities between their national settings. Carnegie and Rockefeller succeeded first in the United States, then the world's largest single free market; their horizons were not always international. They were among America's pioneering builders of "big business," a new, modern institution combining many business functions in one organization and soon requiring skilled management from professional persons.

When Siemens went into business, however, Germany was not yet a nation-state. The institutional or organizational nature of his business was very different from that of the giant firms that evolved from the activities of Americans like Carnegie and Rockefeller. Siemens engaged in international activities from an early stage in his business career. Almost from the start his firm was multinational. The Siemens firm, in contrast to those beginning to dominate the American economy at the time, was old-fashioned in an organizational or institutional sense. "The House of Siemens" is an apt phrase to describe it, because kinship ties were central to its functioning. Werner von Siemens as an entrepreneur was the head of a house who worked with and through his brothers and other relatives, or closely trusted partners, for much of his career. It was not until Werner neared retirement that his firm began to change to a more modern legal and institutional form.

What follows is thus a fascinating story for the English-speaking reader unfamiliar with all the dimensions of Werner von Siemens's life. It is the story of an important German industrialist whose inventions have helped to change our lives. It is the story of the founding of a firm whose scope is broad indeed and whose activities a century after its founder's death affect the well-being of peoples around the world.

K. Austin Kerr
Mansel G. Blackford

Preface

The present publication is part of a long-term research program on the history of the Siemens Corporation and the development of the German electrical industry and was initiated on the occasion of the 100th anniversary of the death of Werner von Siemens. The purpose is less an analysis of the technical achievements accomplished—a field other scholars have already extensively explored—than a review of the enterprising spirit and importance of the founder of the Telegraph System Construction Enterprise Siemens & Halske. The history of this business firm, which formed the nucleus of the present Siemens Corporation, parallels to a large extent the development of the German electrical industry. For valuable support in the preparation of this book I am deeply indebted to my present or former assistants Jost Schmidt, Ruth Vornefeld, Almuth Bartels, and Robert Harring, and particularly to Dr. Herbert Goetzeler, the long-term director of the Siemens Museum in Munich, Germany.

Wilfried Feldenkirchen
Nuremberg, September 1992

I owe special thanks to Mansell Blackford and especially to K. Austin Kerr, the editors of the series, who have not only edited this book but have been a tremendous help in preparing it for an American reader. The translation has been done by Bernhard Steinebrunner.

1994

Chronology

Year	Major Events in Siemens's Life and Business	Related Milestones in Science and Technology
1816	Werner Siemens born	
1818		L. G. Brugnatelli dies, Italian chemist who gilded metals by electrolysis as early as 1805
1819		James Watt dies, inventor of the first practical steam engine, patented 1769
1820		H. C. Ørsted (1777–1851) discovers magnetic effect of electric current
		A.-M. Ampère (1775–1836) investigates electrodynamic interaction of current conductors
1821		Michael Faraday (1791–1867) discovers the basic principle of the electric motor
1822		J. B. J. Fourier (1768–1830) proposes his "analytical theory of heat"
1823	Brother Wilhelm born	
1824		Sadi Carnot (1796–1832) publishes his fundamental ideas on thermodynamics (Carnot cycle)

Year	Major Events in Siemens's Life and Business	Related Milestones in Science and Technology
1825		William Sturgeon (1783–1850) constructs the first electromagnet able to support more than its own weight
1826	Brother Friedrich born (d. 1904)	G. S. Ohm (1789–1854) develops his theory of electrical conduction (Ohm's law)
		Unter den Linden in Berlin illuminated with gas lighting
1829	Brother Carl born (d. 1906)	
1830		Inauguration of a steam railway line between Liverpool and Manchester
1831		Faraday formulates the law of electromagnetic induction
1832	Werner attends a Gymnasium in Lübeck (until 1834)	C. F. Gauss (1777–1855) publishes a treatise on the theory of geomagnetism
		Faraday introduces the already known concept of lines of force as a physical model
1833	Brother Walter born	Gauss and W. Weber (1808–91) build and operate an electromagnetic needle telegraph
		Charles Babbage (1792–1871) builds a program-controlled calculating machine, a forerunner of today's computer
1834		M. H. von Jacobi (1801–74) constructs the first practical electric motor
1835	Werner begins officers' training at the Artillery and Engineering Academy in Berlin	First German railway built between Nuremberg and Fürth

Year	Major Events in Siemens's Life and Business	Related Milestones in Science and Technology
1836		J. F. Daniell (1790–1845) constructs an improved electric cell
1837		Charles Wheatstone (1802–75) and W. F. Cook patent an early model of the electric telegraph
		Samuel Morse (1791–1872) and C. A. von Steinheil (1801–70) independently construct an electromagnetic telegraph
1838	Werner receives his commission in the Prussian Army	First Prussian railway line from Berlin to Potsdam inaugurated
1839	The brothers' mother, Eleonore (b. 1792), née Deichmann, dies	L. J. M. Daguerre (1787–1851) takes out a patent on the photographic technique developed jointly with J. N. Niepce (1765–1833) (daguerreotype)
1840	The brothers' father, Christian Ferdinand (b. 1787), dies; Werner assumes responsibility for his many younger brothers and sisters	J. P. Joule (1818–89) formulates the heating effect of electric current
1841	In addition to his duties as an army officer, Werner increasingly devotes himself to scientific and technical problems	Robert Bunsen (1811–99) invents the carbon-zinc electric cell (Bunsen cell)
1842	Werner awarded his first patent, on a gold electroplating process	J. R. Mayer (1814–78) formulates the principle of conservation of energy
1843	Wilhelm travels to England and sells Werner's gold-plating process	Wheatstone invents the Wheatstone bridge, a device that accurately measures electrical resistance
1844	Wilhelm moves permanently to England	Morse sets up the first long-distance electric telegraph line, from Washington, D.C., to Baltimore

Year	Major Events in Siemens's Life and Business	Related Milestones in Science and Technology
1845	Werner and his future partner Johann Georg Halske (1814–90) become founding members of the Physical Society in Berlin	Gustav Kirchhoff (1824–87) formulates laws describing the branching of current in systems of electric conductors
1846	Convinced of the great importance of electrical telegraphy, Werner resolves to devote himself to it professionally	
1847	Werner invents important improvements to the Wheatstone pointer telegraph; he and Halske (along with Werner's cousin Johann Georg Siemens) then found the Siemens & Halske (S & H) Telegraph Construction Enterprise in Berlin Werner designs a press for covering wire with gutta-percha, important for insulating underground cables	H. Helmholtz (1821–94) extends the law of conservation of energy to electricity Thomas Alva Edison born (d. 1931)
1848	Werner remains in the army during the period of political instability surrounding the March revolution; he has been joined in Berlin by Friedrich, Carl, and Walter, who finish their schooling there S & H begins construction on the first electrical long-distance telegraph line in Europe, from Berlin to Frankfurt (completed in 1849)	
1849	Having received an honorable discharge from the army, Werner is now able to devote himself totally to S & H Wilhelm begins work at Fox & Henderson in Birmingham, where he is later joined by Friedrich	A. H. L. Fizeau (1819–96) measures the speed of light with the aid of a rotating toothed wheel

Year	Major Events in Siemens's Life and Business	Related Milestones in Science and Technology
	Carl joins S & H in Berlin as a designer of telegraph lines	
	S & H helps to found a health and death benefit fund for machine construction workers in Berlin	
1850	Wilhelm takes over the London branch of S & H	First submarine telegraph cable laid, from Dover to Calais, using gutta-percha insulated cables
1851	The company supplies 75 pointer telegraphs for the Russian telegraph line from St. Petersburg to Moscow	William Thomson (1824–1907), later Lord Kelvin, introduces the term *energy*
	S & H builds first electric fire alarm system for Berlin	
	S & H awarded the Council Medal, the highest distinction, at the Crystal Palace Exhibition in London	
1852	Carl forced to close unsuccessful S & H subsidiary in Paris	In the U.S., the word *telegram* is proposed for telegraphically transmitted messages
	S & H in Berlin moves into a factory in Markgrafenstraße	
	Werner marries Mathilde Drumann; he travels to St. Petersburg for the first time	
1853	Werner's son Arnold born (d. 1918)	The last optical telegraph lines in Germany and France are closed down
	The company starts construction of the Russian state telegraph network; Carl moves to St. Petersburg as S & H's representative	

Year	Major Events in Siemens's Life and Business	Related Milestones in Science and Technology
1854	Werner and Carl Frischen (1830–90), independently of one another, announce the invention of a suitable telegraphy circuit for electromagnetic duplex operation	H. Goebel (1818–93) constructs a carbon filament lamp in New York
1855	Werner's son Wilhelm born (d. 1919) Russian subsidiary founded under Carl in St. Petersburg; the Russian business has expanded during the Crimean War (1853–56)	H. Bessemer (1813–98) invents an economical method of steel manufacture
1856	Werner invents the H armature and uses it in a pointer telegraph with a magneto (railway telegraph) Friedrich develops the regenerative furnace, important for the manufacture of glass and steel	The Association of German Engineers founded in Alexisbad (Harz)
1857	Werner develops a better method of submarine cable laying	
1858	"Inventory bonuses" (a profit-sharing scheme) instituted at Siemens The London subsidiary becomes independent under the name Siemens, Halske, & Co., with Wilhelm as director	C. W. Field (1819–92) lays the first transatlantic telegraph cable, which is operational for only a few weeks
1859	Werner and Wilhelm appointed personal advisers to the British government on deep-sea cables Wilhelm marries Anne Gordon (1821–1901), becomes a British citizen, and changes his name to William	F. de Lesseps (1805–94) begins construction of Suez Canal, which is not completed until 1869 Kirchhoff and Bunsen develop the theory of chemical spectral analysis

Year	Major Events in Siemens's Life and Business	Related Milestones in Science and Technology
1860	The University of Berlin awards Werner an honorary doctorate Werner suggests a mercury resistance standard (Siemens unit)	J. J. E. Lenoir (1822–1900) designs a practical, though as yet uneconomical, gas motor First telegraph line to India completed
1861	Werner is cofounder of the German Progressive party	P. Reis (1834–74) constructs an electrical telephone
1862	Werner becomes a member of the Prussian parliament (until 1866) Wilhelm elected a fellow of the British Royal Society	
1863	As a member of the council of the Berlin Chamber of Commerce, Werner writes memorandum entitled "Positive Suggestions Relating to a Patent Law" The first Siemens cable factory established in Woolwich, England	Permanent electric beacon set up at Cape La Hève near Le Havre World's first underground steam railway starts operation in London
1864	Failure of the Cartagena-Oran cable-laying project Acquisition of the Kedabeg copper mine in the Caucasus by Carl First production of Siemens-Martin steel by the process developed by Wilhelm and P. E. Martin (1824–1915) of France	
1865	The English Siemens subsidiary is restructured under the name Siemens Brothers Werner's wife, Mathilde, dies	First German horse-drawn tramway, in Berlin

Year	Major Events in Siemens's Life and Business	Related Milestones in Science and Technology
1866	Werner discovers the principle of the self-excited generator and constructs the first dynamo	First continually operational transatlantic telegraph cable, laid by C. W. Field, starts operation
1867	Halske retires from the management of S & H	George Westinghouse (1846–1914) develops a compressed air brake for railways
	Carl leaves St. Petersburg, settling first in Tbilisi	
	At the fourth world exhibition in Paris, Werner proposes the idea of an electrically operated elevated railway for Berlin's city center	
1868	Walter, now serving as the brothers' negotiator in Tehran, dies in an accident. Their nephew Georg Siemens, later a director of Deutsche Bank, replaces him	
	Foundation of emergency relief fund for S & H employees	
	Construction begins on the Indo-European telegraph line	
1869	After the death of his wife, Carl moves to London and promotes the development of the Siemens subsidiary there	D. Mendeleyev (1834–1907) and J. L. Meyer (1830–95) independently establish the periodic table of chemical elements
1870	Inauguration of Indo-European telegraph line from London to Calcutta (under construction since 1868)	
	Orders from the Prussian military increase, in response to the Franco-Prussian War (1870–71)	
	The Siemens company now employs more than 1,000 people in Germany and abroad	

Year	Major Events in Siemens's Life and Business	Related Milestones in Science and Technology
1871	Introduction of electromechanical blocking system for railways, developed by the engineer Carl Frischen, who has worked for Siemens since 1869	
1872	Werner's youngest son, Carl Friedrich, born (d. 1941)	
	Siemens engineer Friedrich von Hefner-Alteneck (1845–1904) builds a drum armature for dynamos	
	Founding of a pension fund for Siemens employees in Berlin, London, and St. Petersburg	
1873	Werner becomes a member of Berlin's Royal Prussian Academy of Sciences	James Clerk Maxwell (1831–79) publishes his treatises on electricity and magnetism
	Cable factory at Woolwich expanded	
	Johann Sigmund Schuckert (1846–95) founds an electromechanical workshop in Nuremberg—the core of the future Schuckert company, which in 1903 merges with Siemens	
1874	The company's ship *Faraday* starts laying a transatlantic telegraph cable from Ireland to the U.S. (completed 1875)	
1875	Werner proposes the principle of an optical-electrical selenium cell	

Year	Major Events in Siemens's Life and Business	Related Milestones in Science and Technology
1876	Germany passes a new patent law, partly in response to lobbying efforts by Werner	Alexander Graham Bell (1847–1922) designs and demonstrates a workable telephone
	Wilhelm visits Niagara Falls and suggests that its water power should be used to generate electricity	Nikolaus Otto (1832–91) builds a four-stroke internal combustion engine, the first practical alternative to the steam engine
	S & H opens its own cable factory in Berlin	
1877	Werner becomes member of the State Patent Office, founded at his initiative	Edison builds a cylinder phonograph
1878	Werner makes fundamental improvements to the telephone	D. E. Hughes (1831–1900) designs carbon microphone
	Differential arc lamp designed by Hefner-Alteneck ready for production	First elevated railway, in New York (with steam locomotives)
	Start of mass production of dynamos	
1879	Siemens demonstrates the first electric railway (with external power supply) at the Berlin industrial exhibition	Edison builds a carbon filament lamp and subsequently designs the power supply system for household lighting
	Siemens subsidiary founded in Vienna by Arnold, Werner's eldest son	
	Werner helps found the Electrotechnical Society in Berlin, together with Heinrich von Stephan (1831–97), the postmaster general	
1880	Siemens constructs first electric elevator, in Mannheim, and proposes an electrical elevated railway for Berlin	

Year	Major Events in Siemens's Life and Business	Related Milestones in Science and Technology
	Carl returns to St. Petersburg, and the Russian branch of the business becomes independent	
1881	Siemens Brothers, London, becomes a public company	Inauguration of first Berlin telephone exchange
	Siemens builds the first electric tramway in Lichterfelde, near Berlin	Edison demonstrates his incandescent lamp at the First International Electrical Exhibition, held in Paris
	In a lecture before the Berlin Electrotechnical Society, Werner suggests that departments of electrical engineering be set up at technical universities	
	S & H completes state telegraph cable network (jointly with Felten & Guilleaume), in construction since 1877	
1882	The company opens a cable factory in St. Petersburg	First public electricity-generating plants start operation in London (Holborn Viaduct) and New York (Pearl Street)
	Siemens uses an electric locomotive for a coal mine at Zaukeroda in Saxony	
	Siemens builds the first trolley bus system in Berlin; it also installs the first permanent electrical street lighting in Berlin with differential arc lamps (Potsdamer Platz, Leipziger Straße)	
1883	The company begins local production in Vienna	German Edison Company for Applied Electricity (DEG, later called AEG) founded by Emil Rathenau (1838–1915)
	Wilhelm knighted Sir William by Queen Victoria; he dies in the same year	

Year	Major Events in Siemens's Life and Business	Related Milestones in Science and Technology
1884	S & H obtains a German patent on coaxial cable, used in telephones	
	The Russian branch wins great prestige by floodlighting Nevsky Prospekt	
1885	Arnold's son Hermann born (d. 1986)	Galileo Ferraris (1847–97) undertakes rotary field experiments, eventually making possible the development of the asynchronous self-starting electric motor
	Uniform guidelines finally established for the company's sales representatives	
	Stained-glass window in Westminster Abbey dedicated to Wilhelm	Berlin's first central power station starts operation in the Markgrafenstraße
1886	Werner awarded honorary doctorate by University of Heidelberg and appointed knight of the order of merit for sciences and arts	G. Daimler (1834–1900) and C. F. Benz (1844–1929) build the first petrol-driven motor car
	Accumulator-powered Spree boat *Elektra* demonstrated by S & H	
	Hefner-Alteneck and C. Hoffmann (1844–1910) develop the internal-pole direct current machine	
	S & H's St. Petersburg Society for Electrical Lighting founded as a public corporation	
1887	The Physical-Technical State Institute is founded in Berlin, at Werner's suggestion and with his help	E. Berliner (1851–1929), a German emigrant to America, replaces phonograph cylinders with a circular disk, the record; he calls the player a gramophone
1888	Werner raised to Prussian hereditary peerage by Kaiser Friedrich III	In his paper "On Radiation of Electrical Energy," H. R. Hertz (1857–94) describes his successful experiments with electromagnetic waves and proves Maxwell's electromagnetic theory correct
	First appointment of a factory doctor at S & H	

Year	Major Events in Siemens's Life and Business	Related Milestones in Science and Technology
1889	Siemens engineer Walter Reichel (1867–1937) constructs bow collector for railways, enabling the company to enter the electric streetcar business Edison visits Werner in Berlin	Herman Hollerith (1860–1929) is granted a patent on his automatic punched card counting machine (registered 1884), an important precursor of the electronic computer M. von Dolivo-Dobrowolsky (1862–1919) builds the first three-phase asynchronous motor
1890	Werner hands the company over to his brother Carl and his sons Arnold and Wilhelm; S & H becomes a limited partnership Johann Georg Halske dies in Berlin The first Technical Office of the Berlin company is opened in Munich	World's first electrical underground railway built, in London
1891	S & H introduces the 8.5-hour working day (50-hour week), a pioneering step in social policy	Long-distance transmission of electrical energy (three-phase current) realized between Lauffen am Neckar and Frankfurt, site of the International Electrotechnical Exhibition (approx. 175 km) Construction of the Trans-Siberian railway line starts
1892	Arnold travels to America and founds the S & H Electric Company of America in Chicago, but production is later abandoned when the factory is destroyed by fire First three-phase power station built by Siemens at Erding (Upper Bavaria) Werner dies in Berlin-Charlottenburg shortly after completing his memoirs	First automatic telephone exchange opened in La Porte, Indiana, using selectors designed by the American inventor A. B. Strowger (1839–1902)

Introduction

The story of Werner von Siemens (1816–92) is an important part of the history of industrialization in Germany. Siemens played a key role in German industrialization as an inventor and, especially, as an entrepreneur with a broad and international business vision. He worked successfully to take German technology to other countries. The result was the founding of a profitable business enterprise that bore his name, that continued his approach of combining entrepreneurial and international vision with technological innovation, and that stood at the end of the twentieth century as one of the largest industrial firms in the world.

Industrialization began in Germany in the middle of the 1830s, and the processes of industrial change accelerated around 1850. Before industrialization, the German economy was largely agricultural and less prosperous than other economies of western Europe, and certainly less vigorous than the economy of Britain, where industrialization first began to appear in the late eighteenth century. With industrialization, however, combined with political union after 1870, the German economy boomed, and Germany became one of the world's economic powers.

Werner von Siemens's prominence in German industrialization resulted from his participation as an inventor and entrepreneur in electrical technology. During his lifetime,

1

industrialization in Germany went through two phases. The first phase saw the construction of railway lines, the growth of new technologies in mechanical engineering, and the appearance of heavy industry, especially iron and steel. The second phase took place at the end of the nineteenth century. Sometimes called the "second industrialization," it took a rather dynamic course in Germany as compared with other nations. The increasing utilization of electricity and of newly developed inorganic and organic chemical products were the predominant characteristics of the "second industrialization" in Germany. Both the electrical and the chemical industries were fundamental innovations, as defined by the Austrian economist Josef Schumpeter,[1] fostered by technical progress in science and engineering. Although by 1914 the production value of these "new" industrial branches and their share of the total number of employees were still minor in comparison with "traditional" industries, electrical and chemical goods were enjoying above average growth rates and had obvious potential for substantial expansion.

Siemens was an electrical engineer who developed several inventions that proved highly profitable. He was first acclaimed in the field of telegraphy, and founded a firm, Siemens & Halske, that built Germany's first important telegraph line and that went on to build telegraph lines elsewhere in Europe and in Asia. Siemens learned how to insulate wires with guttapercha, a natural latex from the *Palaquium gutta* tree in Malaysia, and this invention allowed his firm to be a pioneer in laying underground and submarine telegraph cables. The most dramatic among Werner von Siemens's many inventions was the modern electric dynamo, which made possible the inexpensive generation of electricity.

The Development of Electrical Engineering

The electrical engineering projects and the business of supplying electrical goods in which Siemens participated had their origins in breakthroughs in scientific knowledge about electricity. The theory of electricity developed as a science at the end of the eighteenth century from the observation and interpretation of physical phenomena. The study of electricity represented an entirely new field of physics, theretofore dominated by the study of mechanics and the initial investigations of thermodynamics. Within two centuries the basic laws concerning electricity were discovered and investigated. Engineers learned how to apply electricity as a practical form of energy. The new product technology associated with electricity escalated rapidly, and the financial benefits of using electricity led investors to adopt its technology. Just as the overall process of economic growth since the middle of the nineteenth century was self-supporting owing to the primary and secondary effects of income and capacity, so too was the development of the electrical industry driven by multiplying opportunities in its product technology. Siemens and others invented, improved, and manufactured machines and instruments for the production, storage, transmission, and transformation of electrical energy into other forms of useful energy.[2]

Once the basic principles of electrical energy were understood, Siemens and others discovered and explored new possibilities of and applications for electricity. Consequently, by the end of the twentieth century electrical engineering came to be, directly or indirectly, intimately connected with all spheres of daily life. Growth in the world market for electrical and electronic products and services has been positive throughout this period. With a value of $1,712 billion in 1993, the world market in electrical and electronic equipment is one of the largest, and with a 12% share of manufacturing, the electrical industry is the second largest industrial branch.

Before 1780, observers knew electricity merely as a curiosity, as something generated by rubbing glass rods or sulphur spheres with silk or wool, what was later called "static electricity." Observation of the electricity generated by this rubbing, and of lightning and magnetism, increasingly aroused the curiosity of many philosophers and physicists in the second half of the eighteenth century, the Age of Enlightenment. Electrotechnical experiments resulted in the discovery of new phenomena, some of which could soon be put to practical use. A major breakthrough occurred in 1780 when Luigi Galvani (1737–98) discovered contact electricity. Further contributions soon appeared: Charles-Augustin de Coulomb (1736–1806) discovered a law, named after him, describing the forces of attraction and repulsion of electrical charges. The lightning rod invented by Benjamin Franklin (1706–90) is still in use today. Georg Simon Ohm (1789–1854) was the first to express the relations between electrical current, voltage, and resistance in a law, which was to bear his name. André-Marie Ampère (1775–1836) established a law on the interaction between two parallel conductors carrying electrical currents. Hans Christian Ørsted (1777–1851), while analyzing the effects associated with continuous (direct) current, observed the declination of a magnetic needle by an electrical current. His discovery of the mutual interaction between electric and magnetic fields made him the founder of the science of electromagnetism.

In the following decades the Englishmen Michael Faraday (1791–1867) and James Clerk Maxwell (1831–79) systematically developed the experimental foundations of electrical engineering.[3] Faraday found out that a voltage was generated when a conductor or a coil was moved in a magnetic field (induction).[4] This discovery enabled the use of electricity as a practical form of energy. Maxwell confirmed the mutual relations between an electrical current and a magnetic field discovered by Ørsted and Faraday. In addition, he devised equations, named after him, which provided the theoretical-mathematical tools for subsequent practitioners.

Although the principle of electromagnetic induction made the transformation of mechanical into electrical energy feasible, its practical use was still limited. Galvanic elements could not be produced in any size, and the magnetic-electrical machines using induction to generate electrical power needed large permanent magnets, which proved difficult to produce and which, in addition, reduced the efficiency of the machines.[5]

For these reasons the beginnings of the electrical industry were identical with the development of low-current technol-

Michael Faraday (1791–1867)

ogy, as signal transmission technology was called at that time to distinguish it from electrical power technology. The first products of the low-current technology "industry," which during the early stages was still based on a centralized workshop type of production, were the electrical telegraph, the overhead lines, and the cable for long distance telecommunication.[6] The development of the first electrical industry was made possible by the improvements to the telegraph made in 1837 by the American Samuel Morse. Morse constructed the first electrical telegraph producing a line in zigzag writing at the receiving station. His system soon replaced the existing optical systems, based on stations on hills using semaphore, and proved superior to the pointer type electrical telegraph invented by Charles Wheatstone. The system developed by Morse was able to meet the rapidly increasing demand for information and communication systems as the world economy developed. In his system direct current, provided by galvanic elements and switched on in short and longer intervals in the rhythm of Morse code, served as the medium of communication.

Werner von Siemens:
Inventor and Businessman

Werner von Siemens was among the leading personalities who created the conditions for the development of electrical technology from the initial experimental stage into the modern electrical industry. From 1888 on, after he had been granted hereditary nobility, he bore the name Werner von Siemens, a name virtually synonymous with the early stages of German electrical technology.[7] Siemens's prominence—and the importance of the enterprise Siemens & Halske, founded by him in 1847 and the nucleus of the present Siemens Corporation—has attracted the attention of biographers and of historians of industrial economy and of technology. A short time after Werner's death, and under the supervision of his younger brother Carl, Richard Ehrenberg began a study entitled "The Enterprises of the Siemens Brothers" ("Die Unternehmungen der Brüder Siemens"). This work was never completed; the first volume alone was published in 1906. On the occasion of Werner's 100th birthday, Conrad Matschoß published a short description of his "life and accomplishments" ("Leben und Werk") in conjunction with a partial edition of his letters. In 1966, as part of the activities for the 150th birthday of the founder of German electrical technology, Sigfrid von Weiher published a synopsis of the publications mentioned above, and of numerous specialized studies that had been prepared in the meantime.[8]

The scholarly exploration of Werner von Siemens's life and accomplishments has emphasized primarily his importance in the technological development of electrical engineering. This emphasis is appropriate, considering Siemens's pioneering inventions and developments, such as the pointer telegraph and the discovery of the dynamo-electric principle—to mention only the most important. The impact of his achievements in the nineteenth century might well be compared to the rapid advancements in microelectronics in the twentieth century. Because of Siemens's outstanding contributions to technology, his importance as a businessman has received less attention, despite the fact that his activities as a businessman promoted the development of the electrical industry in a decisive way. Notwithstanding his strong interest in technology, Werner von Siemens until the last years of his life expended much effort on the acquisition of profitable enterprises that would enhance the prestige of his firm. Many of these enterprises were engaged not only in production but also in the installation and operation of industrial plants.[9]

Werner von Siemens left his mark as a businessman and as an inventor. In that respect he differed from Wheatstone and Morse, whose contributions were limited to science and invention. Unlike those two important contemporaries, Siemens provided a synthesis between science and business, establishing the business philosophy of the Siemens company that persists to the present day. Siemens's approach, and the approach of the company that bears his name more than a century after his death, may be summed up as the use of the technical and economic possibilities of electricity in a general and universal sense, concentrating almost exclusively on electrical engineering and electronics. Siemens the man and Siemens the company were involved in almost the entire spectrum of electrical technology, including activities and representation in all the world's markets.[10]

As a businessman, Siemens combined the qualities of the entrepreneur and the manager. Recent research on the concept of entrepreneurship considers an entrepreneur as distinct from a manager in that an entrepreneur makes decisions of strategic importance that transcend the mere managerial level of a firm. In addition, an entrepreneur differs from a capitalist in that his own stake in the capital of the enterprise is of secondary importance to his position. For a long time Werner von Siemens engaged personally in managerial tasks in his firm and, after the first consolidation, became the most important contributor of its capital. Entrepreneurial activities, however, were always of primary concern to him.

The established scholarship on Siemens stressing his role as an inventor reflects his own wishes. He wanted to be seen as a scientist and inventor. Siemens never showed great interest in or particular esteem for the profession of a businessman.[11] In spite of his predilections, however, Siemens's own writings, both published and unpublished, reveal a man with a business vision and the ability to carry out that vision. For instance, the treatise "On the Transformation of Mechanical Power into Electrical Current without the Application of Permanent Magnets," which Siemens submitted to the Academy of Sciences of Berlin on January 17, 1867, reveals him to be not only a scientist trying to get to the bottom of the observed phenomena but also an engineer and farsighted businessman deducing, from his experiences with his experimental machine, the following prediction: "At present, technology has acquired the means to generate electric currents of unlimited strength in an inexpensive and convenient way at any place where mechanical power is available. This fact will be of utmost importance in several of its branches."[12]

Werner von Siemens outlined his expectations for his invention in even greater detail in a letter to his brother Wilhelm in England, dated December 4, 1866: "Provided the design is correct, the effects should turn out to be enormous. This concept can well be expanded and may initiate a new era in electromagnetism. Thus magnetic electricity will become available very inexpensively, and lighting, galvanometallurgy, etc., even small electromagnetic machines obtaining their energy from larger ones may become feasible and useful."[13] At this early stage, Werner von Siemens already envisioned the principal applications for electric power that were in general use by the time of his death. This vision, combined with Siemens's business acumen, led to the creation of a significant industry. When Siemens died in 1892, Siemens & Halske alone produced 1,000 electric generators annually, had sales of almost 20 million marks, and employed 6,500 persons worldwide, 4,775 of whom worked in Germany.

The Enterprise Siemens & Halske

For the most part, historians of the many firms of the Siemens Corporation have focused on the history of the firm Siemens & Halske in Berlin. But such an approach overlooks the fact that the business strategy of Werner von Siemens was internationally oriented. This strong international orientation was apparent even before the foundation of the Telegraph System Construction Enterprise in 1847, and it continued as the existence of the Berlin business came to be based almost exclusively upon its foreign relationships. Indeed, the growth of the foreign branches occasionally outpaced the parent enterprise in Berlin. The international orientation and the corporate identity of the present Siemens Corporation dates back to the spirit of the founder. Ever since its founding, the firm has been a European enterprise while retaining characteristic German features. At the end of the 1870s this international orientation was emphasized by the establishment of a production plant in Austria, and since 1890 by the creation of Siemens Technical Offices at home and abroad. During Siemens's lifetime, only a few other German businessmen showed a determination comparable to that of Werner and his brothers in regard to the establishment of branches in other European countries.

Against this background, the present study, which was initiated on the occasion of the 100th anniversary of Werner von Siemens's death on December 6, 1892, focuses on the most important strategic decisions for the development of the multinational Siemens enterprise, on the specific reasons for the engagement abroad, and on the international marketing strategies pursued. This emphasis on business activities is not intended to detract from Siemens's achievements as a scientist, technician, and inventor, particularly since they formed the basis for his social and economic rise. The obvious economic success of the enterprises of Werner von Siemens and his brothers at home and abroad, however, justifies an approach investigating the reasons for this success grounded both in the circumstances of the time and in the personalities of the founder of the business and his brothers.

In recent years multinational corporations, operating on a worldwide scale, have attracted both scholarly and public attention. Anglo-American scholars in particular have asked why such enterprises developed and what influences they have had on the international economic web. Case studies have shown that enterprises on their way to becoming international concerns pass through various stages of development: During the first stage of export orientation, independent agents sell the products of the firm abroad. During the second stage, the firm acquires an export agency or hires an export manager. In the course of the expansion of this agency, the enterprise establishes a sales branch or a subsidiary abroad before finally, in the third stage, starting production abroad.

The forerunner firms of the present Siemens Corporation did not follow this three-stage pattern. However, the idea that the expansion of the international network of the Siemens firms in Berlin, London, and St. Petersburg was more similar to the model of the ties of the preindustrial French Huguenot families of bankers and merchants than to the concept of a multinational enterprise is also not correct.[14] With their first inventions and economic enterprises, Werner von Siemens and his brothers strove for success outside of Germany. By starting subsidiaries and manufacturing establishments of their own almost without delay after the founding of the parent firm in Berlin, Siemens met an important criterion of the multinational enterprise.[15]

Part of the explanation for the international orientation of the firm from its beginning most likely involves the special conditions facing the still young electrical "industry" around the middle of the nineteenth century. The electrical industry, and also the chemical industry, were eager to have a presence abroad for the sake of securing patent rights. Furthermore, the special nature of the first electrotechnical products, such as telegraph systems, made an early engagement abroad necessary. These systems, after proving to be of great use, faced a rapidly increasing demand that was neither directly market oriented nor dependent on general economic development but dominated by a few, mostly large governmental or semigovernmental, customers. Another main reason for the engagement abroad is rooted in the personalities of the Siemens brothers—their views, their political convictions, and their strong family ties.

The plans, conflicts, and views of the founder of the firm and his brothers, who also had a share in the business, can be readily traced thanks to the rich treasure of sources available. After his withdrawal from active business, Werner von Siemens wrote his memoirs, a prime source of information. The publication first appeared in 1892, shortly before his death, and is currently available in its eighteenth edition, with an expert introduction.[16] Even allowing for the possibility that a retrospective view on a successful life might describe conflicts in a more favorable light, this autobiography gives important insights into Werner von Siemens's motives and guiding principles.

After the untimely death of Werner's younger brother Wilhelm (1823–83), who had spent almost all of his professional life in England, Wilhelm's widow, Anna, had William Pole write an "official" biography. For this assignment the author had at his disposal Wilhelm's official papers and his notes and letters, as well as oral statements from his wife and friends. Thus this contemporary biography represents an important source of information, although the author largely omitted problems or conflicts among the brothers.

The correspondence between Werner and his brothers undoubtedly offers much insight into their subjective assessments of different situations, plans, and feelings. For decades, the "senior" Werner, who had his residence mostly in Berlin, conducted an exceedingly active correspondence, which lasted almost continuously for over forty years and includes more than five thousand letters. These letters cover everything that

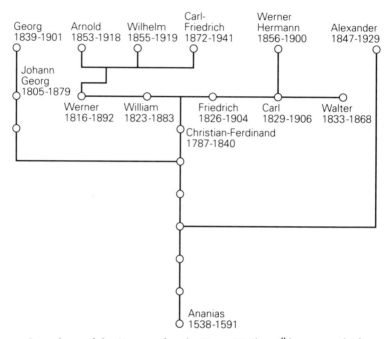

Genealogy of the Siemens family. From Weiher, *Überseegeschäft.*

occupied the brothers with respect to scientific, business, and personal matters; most of them are accessible in transcribed form in the Siemens Archives in Munich, Germany.[17] This wealth of information offers a valuable supplement to the business documents, which have already been analyzed in several studies of the enterprises in Berlin and abroad.[18] The letters reveal a multifaceted picture of Werner von Siemens as a businessman, complementing the prevailing impression of him as a brilliant technician and inventor.

After a short summary of the general economic conditions in Germany at the time (chap. 1), I have structured the following presentation mostly chronologically. A short outline of Werner's family background, his childhood and youth (as far as they can be reconstructed from the sparse source material), and his fifteen years of military service (chap. 2) is followed by a description of his entrepreneurial activities, divided into two periods (chaps. 3 and 4).

The initial period of growth of the enterprise Siemens & Halske lasted up to the mid-1860s. During this time Werner was active mostly as an inventor and devoted to the precise details of mechanical design. Manufacturing was for the most part based upon manual work. Division of labor or the use of machines occupied only a minor role. The start of the process of the separation from his partner, Johann Georg Halske (1814–90); Werner's changed political engagement (in 1866 his political creed shifted within a few months from a liberal-oppositional view to a national-liberal one in support of Bismarck);[19] and finally the new business possibilities created by electrical power technology, which soon surpassed low-current technology owing to its much wider range of applications, opened up a new period in the firm's history. Manufacturing methods changed; the use of machines, and soon of specialized machines, gained ground rapidly; and problems concerning business had to be solved, in addition to those of technology.

From its beginnings the electrical industry showed an inherent tendency toward large establishments. During the period of development and expansion of telegraph systems this was due to the complicated technology involved, the small number of customers, and their interest in securing a long-term continuous and dependable supply. The tendency toward expansion was enhanced by the high capital requirements of the electric power industry and by the economic recession that Germany experienced at the turn of the century. The economic crisis hit the electric power industry particularly hard, since some parts of that industry operated on a highly speculative basis.

The history of the electric power industry, of course, did not stop with Siemens's death in 1892. The dynamics of the industry eventually produced two large firms that dominated the German market. After the Siemens-Schuckert Corporation gained control of the Bergmann Electrical Corporation in Germany in 1912, two conglomerates of approximately equal weight, Siemens and AEG, faced each other. Together they controlled about 75% of the German market. In some fields of business strong competition prevailed between the two giants, whereas in others they joined forces and occasionally even founded joint subsidiaries, among which Telefunken Corporation was the most important.

Subsequently, in chapter 5, in the form of a short survey, I discuss the most important parameters for the success of the enterprise and the personal style of the founder of the firm. An outline of the development of the Siemens concern up to World War I concludes this book (chap. 6).

1

The German Economy in the Second Half of the Nineteenth Century

The founding and early development of the Siemens & Halske firm, "the history of which also reflects the history of German electrical technology," since "none of the competing firms matched it as regards size, qualification, reputation, business connections, control of the market, and power," took place during the period of high industrialization in Germany and of the development of the world economy.[1] These conditions created the prerequisites for the expansion of the company. In turn, the forms the overall economic development took were decisively influenced by the inventions and the economic activities of Siemens & Halske. Initially investing in the telegraph, Siemens & Halske promoted a telecommunications revolution that allowed businesses to alter their operations in fundamental ways and to generate enormous gains in wealth. The following sketch of the most important features of the German economy in the second half of the nineteenth century provides a framework for understanding the dynamic relationships between the growth of the German economy and the particular contributions of Siemens & Halske to that growth.

15

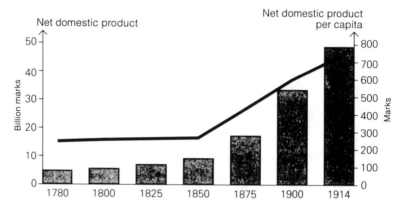

Net domestic product (columns) and net domestic product per capita
(line), 1780–1914

Overall Economic Development in Germany

The industrialization that began in Germany between 1834 and 1849 was marked by several economic, technological, and political features. That fifteen-year period saw the beginning of railroad construction and the establishment of textile companies. Germans designed and constructed new machinery for those industries, and for the coal mining and iron processing businesses as well. Politically, the founding of the German Tariff Union (Deutscher Zollverein) was important, bringing a common market to Germany for the first time. With the foundation laid, German industrialization gathered momentum after 1850. With the exception of the period between 1874 and 1880, the process of growth of the German economy took an uninterrupted course from the middle of the nineteenth century until the outbreak of World War I.

After 1850 economic growth in Germany was much more rapid than it was in England or France. Between 1850 and 1913 the average annual growth rate of the gross domestic product (GDP) in Germany was 2.6%. In part, this spectacular long-term growth was a result of the fact that industrialization began later in Germany than it had in France and England,

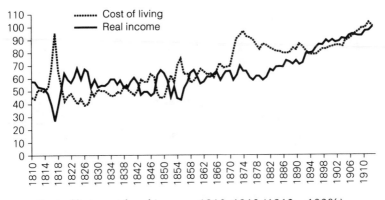

Cost of living and real income, 1810–1913 (1913 = 100%)

and the German economy was therefore "catching up" to more mature neighbors in Europe. The growth in the GDP per capita, with an average annual increase of 1.6%, was also spectacular, all the more so because Germany witnessed an unprecedented population growth from about 35 million people in 1850 to about 67 million in 1913. Industrialization brought about a long-term increase in real income and in the standard of living for the German people. Industrialization, moreover, meant not just that there was a larger volume of goods available for the consumer, but that there were more funds for investment and more goods for export. In sum, the economic growth associated with industrialism was without precedent in Germany.

Economic growth also changed the relationship between agriculture and manufacturing. Paralleling the rapid growth of trade and industry in Germany was a considerable rise of productivity in the primary sector, that is, agriculture and forestry, which had been predominant in the preindustrial period. The growth of agricultural productivity meant that Germany could feed its growing population and release labor for the developing industrial sector. As a result, before World War I the contribution to the GDP by the secondary sector already amounted to more than 45%.

Although at the beginning of the nineteenth century more

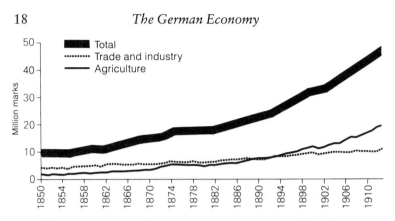

Value added in the German national economy, 1850–1913

than two-thirds of all persons employed worked in agriculture and forestry, this percentage had decreased by the middle of the century to a little over one-half and by 1913 to one-third of the working population, despite an absolute growth of the primary sector that lasted until after the turn of the century. The decreasing percentage of persons employed in the agricultural sector corresponded to an absolute and relative increase of industrially employed persons (the increase in the services sector, which since the 1960s has featured the largest proportion of the total employment, was still lagging far behind).

The growth of industrial production (1913 = 100%)

Industrialization in Germany centered on the capital goods industries, industries that made goods for business customers, not individual consumers. The rise of large-scale enterprises was advanced and accelerated by the development of new financing instruments. The German consumer goods industry did not enjoy such favorable conditions for production and sales as did its English competitors, who in the middle of the nineteenth century dominated the world market with inexpensive products of good quality.

The Role of the Electrical Industry in German Industrialization

The electrical industry, which developed from small-scale enterprises, increasingly contributed to the upward trend in trade and industry. Quantitatively, the initial development in the electrical field cannot be fully substantiated. Government statistics that could illustrate the different stages of the electronics industry in the course of total industrial development are not available until after 1900, and then only for the number of persons employed, some of whom have to be classified instead as belonging to the electrical trades.[2] Governmental surveys on the net output for German industry were not carried out until 1936. As a result, the data on the productivity of the German electrical industry for the years 1890, 1895, 1898, and 1913 are based on estimates and surveys carried out by the electrical industry itself.

Growth of Employment in the Electrical Industry

Year	No. of people employed	Proportion of total no. of people employed in trade and industry (%)
1875	1,157	
1882	1,815	
1895	24,343	0.4
1907	118,963	1.3

The growth of the electrical industry, and consequently its contribution to German economic growth during this period, was quite steady. Political events sometimes intruded on business activity, including the *Gründerkrise,* a business slump that began in 1873 following a bank crash in Vienna that spread to Germany. This slump hardly affected the young electrical sector, however. Business with telegraphs continued on a favorable course, particularly following unification of the general Postal Authority and the Telegraph Office by the new postmaster general, Heinrich von Stephan, in 1875. For 1890 the volume of production of the electrical industry was estimated at 45 million marks.[3]

Then the technology of the industry changed dramatically. The increasing awareness of the enormous technical potential of the three-phase system of alternating current resulted within a few years in a quantum leap in the development of new applications. In 1895 sales amounted to 155 million marks, and in 1898 the value of production already reached 228.7 million marks. The ratio of sales of 211.1 million marks for electrical power products versus 17.6 million marks for low-current equipment illustrates to what extent electrical power technology had changed the character and importance of the electrical industry in general. In 1913 the value of electrotechnical production in Germany was estimated to be 1,300 million marks, a value approximately equaling one-third of the world's electrotechnical production. Germany's share in the world's electrical trade amounted to almost 47%.

Indirectly, the upward trend of the electrical industry was also reflected in the development of the consumption of electric energy. Before 1914 the consumption of electricity was affected above all by the rapid adoption of electric streetcars, which rapidly replaced horse-drawn streetcars after 1890.[4] The changes in the transportation and communication systems, which justify describing the nineteenth century in terms of a "communications revolution," are closely connected with the preconditions and consequences of an economic growth previously unknown for either the German national economy or the global economy.[5] Until 1867 individual postal authori-

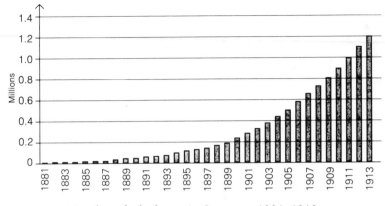

Number of telephones in Germany, 1881–1913

ties existed in the larger German states, but these services were subsequently centralized in a nationally operated and organized postal system entrusted with the monopoly for all telegraph, telephone, and letter mail services. As a consequence, the public services of the German post and telegraph offices increased fiftyfold from 1850 to 1913 and by World War I amounted to almost one-fifth of the value added by all transport services.[6] In addition to the continuing expansion of the electrical telegraph service, the expansion of the telephone network after 1880 contributed substantially to the figures quoted above.[7]

As demand rose for the new telecommunications services, the prices charged for using the telegraph and the telephone went down. The new means of communication contributed decisively to the reduction of the considerable interregional differences in prices for material goods and particularly for services within Germany. The convergence of interest rates in different parts of Germany indicated the general convergence of prices for goods and services fostered by the dramatic changes in communication technology. The new communication facilities had an even greater influence on the development of the international exchange of goods and services, as the speed of telecommunication traffic far exceeded the speed

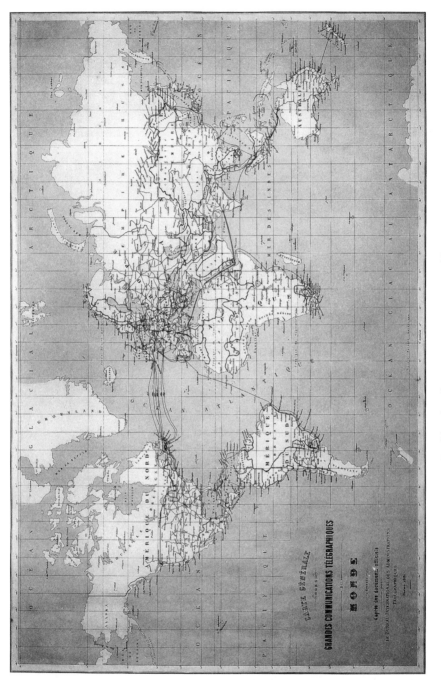

Worldwide telecommunication via cables, 1881

of transporting merchandise.[8] The new systems of communication changed the conduct of economic transactions in a way that precluded the recurrence of economic downturns such as the severe crisis that had beset German agriculture in the 1840s. This crisis proved to be the last of the "old-style" type economic crisis in Germany, a type that the interregional or international exchange of commodities could now prevent.[9]

Germany's Role in World Trade

The volume of world trade grew spectacularly during the same decades in which Germany was undergoing industrialization. The growth of world trade had less to do with the improvements in manufacturing associated with the Industrial Revolution and the growing volume of manufactured goods than with other factors. The idea of free trade, first given full expression by Adam Smith in 1776, spread from England and had an impact on public policies, which led to pressures to reduce tariff barriers and to open markets. The technical innovations of monetary flows and the increasing liberalization of the international exchange of capital created a significant basis for the growth in world trade. The nineteenth-century trade boom was also stimulated by the prevailing period of peace, which was uncommonly long in the history of Europe. One result was the division of labor on an international scale. An international network of trade in products evolved, ultimately resulting in the establishment of prices extending across a worldwide market.

Developments in transportation and communication were central factors in the growth of world trade during the nineteenth century. The development of the railroad and the steamship created reliable systems for moving goods at higher speeds than ever before and at costs that dropped over the long term. The development of the telegraph, and later the telephone, allowed the speedy transmission and processing of orders, the analysis of markets, and the dissemination of market

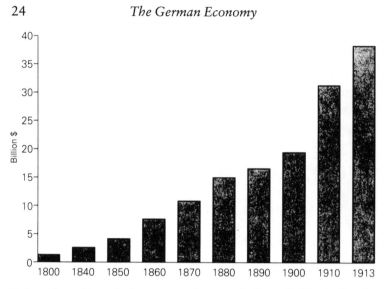

Value of world trade (imports and exports). From Pohl, *Aufbruch*, p. 186.

information. Before the telegraph—capable of carrying messages almost instantaneously over vast distances and across international borders—exporters had been forced to conduct their business through middlemen. Telecommunications changed that situation, allowing exporters to deal directly with international customers. Trading across long distances became more efficient, opening export (and import) opportunities that were unprecedented.

The growth of foreign trade was especially significant for Germany, which by the middle of the nineteenth century was among the world's three leading exporters. The German export trade at the time was mostly in food and raw materials. As worldwide economic connections grew and Germany itself developed from an agricultural into an industrial nation, world trade became increasingly important as an agent of German prosperity. Between 1850 and 1913 German foreign trade increased on the average of 4% annually, even faster than overall economic production. As a result, Germany's share in the volume of world trade had reached 13% in 1913, while the export quota of the German Reich amounted to 17.5% of total industrial production. The increase in the importance of international trade for the German economy was comparatively steady up to World War I, except for fluctuations in the 1870s and 1880s. During the 1870s an economic depression slowed the growth of world trade, whereas during the 1880s protectionism hindered Germany's ability to participate in world trade. Protectionist measures were adopted by many nations in the 1880s, including Germany, which legislated protection for domestic agricultural production by imposing import duties.[10]

Despite the considerable long-term increase in domestic demand, which was further stimulated by the growth in population, after the 1870s German industry became increasingly dependent on the world market. Here the sales returns were mostly lower than on the domestic market, which was protected by tariffs, or sometimes also by cartels or internal agreements.[11]

The organization of the export trade before the telecommunications revolution of the nineteenth century, and the institutions through which it was conducted, had the effect of retarding opportunities for German producers. Before 1850 German export trade was conducted in almost all classes of goods with the help of independent export agencies, unless business deals were concluded at fairs and exhibitions.[12] Trading firms primarily conducted what was an indirect export trade. The trading firms were specialized businesses engaging in the continuous and planned exchange of goods with foreign countries. Located in trade centers, these trading companies typically specialized in one nation's market and sought to satisfy customers in that market. Because of this geographical specialization, the attention of the trader focused less on the goods themselves than on the range of consumers. Particularly in overseas markets, the trader accordingly served more as a buying agent for foreign customers than as a selling agent for German industry. One important result was that the export trade showed little loyalty to particular German products and producers. In many cases German manufacturers sold their export goods under trademarks determined by the trading company, not the manufacturer, leaving the initial producer unknown to the final user and keeping the manufacturer in total dependence on the trader. In this system, furthermore, the range of items traded, mostly consumer goods, was diverse. The trader, not the manufacturer, was responsible for the distribution of German goods abroad, storing them, advertising them, and servicing them. In this situation, there was often little reason for the trading firm to safeguard the interests of the German manufacturer. The livelihood of the trading firm depended on customers in the foreign market, not on the well-being of the German manufacturer. As industrialization progressed, the functions of establishing goods in markets and servicing those goods became more and more important. In particular, the more the share of capital goods in the export business increased, the more unsuitable the existing structure of the export trade proved for export industries. A manufacturer of an electrical machine, for example, found it desirable to have reliable agents abroad who focused on the product, the explanation of its advantages, and its servicing.

As German manufacturers began to replace specialized independent trading firms with agents under their direct control, they also found that having their own offices abroad was advantageous in the face of protectionism. The protectionism that began to take hold in the world economy in the 1880s created obstacles for German exporters, who consequently found it worthwhile to establish their own manufacturing and sales organizations abroad. The great variety of tariff increases repeatedly confronted German industrial enterprises with the question whether it was worth it, under the prevailing conditions, to export goods from Germany into the respective country or whether it would make more sense to move production into the area targeted for sales. Companies within the same branch of an industry reached quite different conclusions in this matter.

Solving the new organizational problems presented by world trade opportunities in the industrial age was not easy. Direct investments abroad were not always regarded as a positive step, for nationalistic reasons. There was also the problem of selecting and delegating employees to post in foreign countries. Stationing employees abroad was usually the first step toward making direct investments in a foreign country. German companies allowed themselves to be guided by a large variety of considerations in any decisions about founding subsidiaries abroad. The increasingly protectionist trade policy around the world constituted the most important consideration, at least in cases where the German firm was not in a position, through a monopoly or other structure, to maintain its share of the market in the face of high import duties.[13] Yet the size of the market, the anticipated development of sales, and the magnitude of the costs involved in a direct investment also had an influence on such a decision. Direct investments contributed to the rise of Germany by the end of the nineteenth century as one of the major creditor nations. For the year 1913 the volume of German direct investments is estimated to have amounted to approximately 10 billion marks and the value of foreign securities held to approximately 20 billion marks. These were significant sums, even if the share of national savings that went into export capital was much lower in Germany than in France or, especially, England.[14]

One of the firms that from the beginning not only methodically strove to sell their products outside German borders but also started production in foreign countries was the Siemens & Halske Company. One important reason for studying the life of Werner von Siemens and the origins of the company that bears his name is to appreciate the multinational character of German business even at an early stage of industrialization.

2

Werner von Siemens's
Early Years

Family Background, Childhood, and Youth

Werner von Siemens was born on December 13, 1816, the child of Christian Ferdinand Siemens and his wife, Eleonore, née Deichmann, at Lenthe, near Hanover in Germany. The marriage was blessed with fourteen children, ten of whom reached adult age, two girls and eight boys. With the exception of the two boys born immediately after Werner, Hans (b. 1818) and Ferdinand (b. 1821), all the brothers cooperated later more or less closely with Werner. The father had leased a country estate and practiced agriculture. The family was a close one, and kinship ties would eventually play a prominent role in Werner's business career.

The Siemens family cannot easily be allocated to a specific social stratum. The family originally came from the Harz Mountains in the region of Goslar and can be traced back to the time of the Thirty Years' War (1618–48). A carefully written chronicle of the family found in the family archives documents middle-class self-confidence. Numerous ancestors held public offices—for example, as members of the town council—and a large percentage had an academic education. Medical doctors, lawyers, and people working in metallurgy can be found in the family background; there were no outstanding talents in technical fields, however. Werner's father had studied agriculture at Göttingen University for several semesters. Werner described him as a well-educated and intelligent gentleman with a wide range of interests whose instructions in world history and ethnology greatly impressed him as a boy at the age of ten. The mother, Eleonore Deichmann, was the daughter of the chief official of Poggenhagen, near Hanover.[1]

Judging by their social background and the liberal-Protestant ethics dominating the family, Werner's parents belonged to the higher educated upper middle class. However, they were not especially prosperous. The poor economic circumstances of the family did not match the relatively high level of education of the parents. When Werner was eight years old, the family left Lenthe after his father had had a dispute with the aristocratic authorities of the Royal British Province of Hanover and leased the country estate Menzendorf in the nearby principality of Ratzeburg (Mecklenburg). The economic situation of the family did not improve with the move. The agricultural crisis of 1818–25—the result of extraordinarily large harvests that depressed prices to rock-bottom levels— damaged the family's fortunes considerably. The income from farming was totally insufficient to meet the cost of taxes, leasing fees, and living expenses,[2] and the large number of children aggravated the family's constant worries about living conditions. Nor did these worries diminish when the agricultural economy improved greatly at the end of the 1820s. The return to prosperity on German farms after 1825 persisted for several decades but did not seem to noticeably improve the fortunes of the Siemens family.

The middle-class ambitions of the family were limited by their straitened financial means. It was especially difficult to provide a formal education for the children. Together with his older sister Mathilde (b. 1814), Werner was at first given lessons by his grandmother, who taught the children how to read and write and made them learn poems by heart. For half a year the father took over the lessons himself, but then sent the eleven-year-old boy to a school in the nearby small town of

Schönberg. When Werner was not particularly successful at that school, his father finally engaged several private teachers, starting at Easter 1829. It was not until the ninth grade that Werner attended a Gymnasium, the Katharinenschule in Lübeck. In retrospect, however, Werner was not very pleased with the predominantly humanistic-classical curricula offered, since he felt that he was not encouraged enough in his true abilities and favorite subjects, particularly mathematics and science. Werner tried to compensate for some of the deficiencies of the school by taking private lessons in mathematics. As early as Easter 1834, at the age of seventeen, he left secondary school for good, without any formal final examination. In the introduction to his memoirs, Werner von Siemens described his career prospects: "It will be informative and encouraging for young people to realize that a young man without inherited wealth or influential sponsors, even without a substantial educational background, can make good progress by his own efforts alone and attain useful achievements."[3]

Although his parents could offer him a school with only limited possibilities, and could not afford a university education commensurate with the talents of their son, Werner later looked back on his childhood and early youth as a period of happiness. The great amount of freedom in the secluded life in the country, an early responsibility for his younger brothers and sisters, and the close family ties were contributing factors. At the same time, his early experience of having to face serious economic problems, which meant that the family's living standard was below that of an ordinary middle-class family, also provided the impetus for Werner to attain some prosperity. Accordingly, he confessed at the age of seventy-one in a letter to his brother Carl:

> I certainly have sought profits and wealth, yet not so much for the purpose of reveling in them, but to obtain the means to fulfill other ideas and ventures and by success win the recognition for the justness of my actions and the usefulness of my

work. It was for that reason that since my youth I have dreamed of founding a worldwide business in the style of the Fugger family in Augsburg, which would provide not only myself but also my descendants with power and reputation all over the world, and assure the financial means to elevate my brothers and sisters and close relatives toward the higher regions of life.[4]

Werner von Siemens's family background was not typical of a businessman of his time. By far most founders of firms either had a mercantile background or came from families with a tradition in a craft or trade.[5] There was almost no profession, however, that did not sprout at least some enterprising spirits during the German industrial revolution. Although Werner was able to gather little practical experience in the management of a company and had practically no family capital at his disposal, his higher than average education certainly played an important role in the course of his later career. The time spent at a grammar school, even though only temporary and not greatly esteemed by Werner because of its emphasis on a humanistic curriculum, was quite untypical for businessmen of his time.

His family background and his education also provided the basis for Werner's often expressed self-identification as a scientist and his distinct middle-class contempt for merchants and mere "money-making people," attitudes that are evident, above all, in the letters to his brother Carl. Werner's attitude reflected the views of the Siemens family, with its noncommercial tradition. His identification of himself as a scientist corresponded, moreover, with the general view of the educated middle class. Academics and civil servants often looked down on technicians and merchants and did not encourage their children to enter such careers.[6] Only as the social respect for the profession of a businessman gradually increased was Werner able to let go of such a negative opinion of commercial and engineering careers.

Professional Training and Military Service

The tight financial situation of Werner's parents limited his opportunities for an advanced education. It was financially impossible for him to attend the Architectural Academy in Berlin, a course of study he had considered. So Werner decided to obtain an education in engineering by joining the Prussian Army. In the spring of 1834, with his father's approval, he left his parents' home in order to walk to Berlin, there to apply for acceptance into the Prussian Engineering Corps.

Upon his arrival in Berlin, Werner showed a high degree of independence and tenacity in the pursuit of his goals. The authorities in Berlin rated his chances for direct admission into the Prussian Engineering Corps fairly low, so they sent him to Magdeburg with a letter of recommendation to apply for acceptance into the artillery brigade. The artillery brigade posted officers to the Artillery and Engineering Academy in Berlin for training. Werner was successful in Magdeburg. Because his classical education had not prepared him with the knowledge of mathematics, physics, geography, and French that the artillery corps required of its officer candidates, Werner studied for the entrance examination for three months. With some luck, he passed the examination. The authorities removed the last obstacle, the fact that he was not a Prussian subject, and admitted him as an artillery officer candidate in December of 1834.

In the autumn of 1835, exactly according to his wishes, Werner von Siemens was assigned to the Artillery and Engineering Academy in Berlin. Here he at last received the thorough training he had longed for. His three-year term of duty at the academy, where the mathematician Georg Simon Ohm, the physicist Heinrich Gustav Magnus, and the chemist Otto Erdmann lectured, and particularly the high-level classes in the fundamental subjects of mathematics, physics, and chemistry, were—according to Werner's own statements—the foundation and prerequisite for his later success. The training at the military academy, which on a scientific level held a position somewhere between a trade school and an engineering college,

Werner von Siemens, 1845

provided him with a clear edge over the majority of technicians with only empirical practical training. After completing the three-year course of studies, Werner received a commission as a lieutenant and obtained his first leave after being away from Menzendorf for over four years.

At home Werner was confronted with the fact that the economic circumstances of his parents had not improved and, even worse, that their health had severely deteriorated. Despite the poor opportunities for earning money, his brothers Hans and Ferdinand had decided to take up agricultural work and were helping their father. The fifteen-year-old Wilhelm was still attending school and, according to his parents' wishes, was to prepare himself to become a merchant. Werner could

Wilhelm Siemens, ca. 1850

not approve such a plan. He decided to take care of his brother and at the end of his leave took Wilhelm with him to Magdeburg, where the boy was to attend a business and trade school.

A year later, when Werner was no longer required to reside in the barracks, he rented an apartment in the city with his friend William Meyer, whom he had met at the academy, and his brother Wilhelm. Thus he was able to look after Wilhelm's training even more intensively. Werner advised Wilhelm to drop mathematics at school in favor of English and began teaching his brother mathematics himself.

Werner's taking charge of Wilhelm's education began a lifetime of close association between the two brothers. The ties between them and also with their younger brothers and sisters grew even closer when their parents died in rapid succession. Their mother died on July 8, 1839, and their father on January

16 the next year. Werner felt responsible for his six younger brothers and sisters, who were still under age and had not finished their education. In the following years Werner always tried to support them financially and be personally involved in their education and professional training.

The close relationship between Werner and Wilhelm soon led to commercial ventures. Werner's military duties left him time for scientific experiments of his own. He particularly made good use of a period of honorary arrest (to which he was sentenced after taking part in a duel as a second), successfully conducting experiments on electrolytic plating with silver and gold. Wilhelm, after leaving school in Magdeburg at Easter 1841, entered Göttingen University, where the husband of their eldest sister, Mathilde, held a chair in chemistry, to pursue scientific studies. For financial reasons Wilhelm had to give up his studies after a short period of time; he then began practical training in engineering in Magdeburg. Wilhelm wearied of engineering training after a few months and at the end of 1842 decided to go traveling and to try to exploit Werner's electroplating inventions commercially.

Wilhelm's first stay in England in the spring and summer of 1843 turned out to be a decisive event for the two brothers. Within a few months he succeeded in applying for a patent for the electrolytic silver- and gold-plating process developed by Werner and in selling it to the English firm Elkington for £1,600 (less £110 for patent fees). This success, which earned them about 30,000 marks, not only helped the brothers to overcome a tight financial situation but also encouraged Wilhelm to consider settling permanently in England. Werner supported this plan, and Wilhelm, after a short stay in Magdeburg in January 1844, accordingly returned to England.

Wilhelm's second trip to England, however, did not produce the quick success of the previous year. Wilhelm, as a twenty-year-old foreigner without any substantial experience, did not have much luck and could not immediately get the knack of English commercial practices. In a letter to Werner he complained bitterly: "I have had the opportunity to hear much about the character of the Englishman and have arrived at the conclusion that it is composed of pure egoism; an Englishman, for example, does not feel any shame in deceiving another person and there is no greater triumph for him than to hoodwink a foreigner, especially a German." In the same letter Wilhelm continued, however, "Yet as a people they are great, because they are free; and the people in Germany cannot imagine what freedom is. When I have lived here for a full year, I will be spoilt for Germany for the rest of my life."[7]

This basic attitude is presumably what led Wilhelm to stay in England, even though for several years his subsequent efforts earned little noteworthy financial reward. The two brothers had to realize that to a large extent the selling of occasional inventions was a gamble. Among the failed projects were, for example, inventions in the field of zincography and a poorly developed machine for fast printing. Apart from trying to sell his brother's inventions, Wilhelm kept himself busy developing some inventions of his own, including a water meter, which in later years turned out to be a very successful product. In the summer of 1844 Werner visited his brother in London and for a few weeks cooperated intensively with him on efforts to develop new inventions. On his way back Werner made a detour via Paris to attend the industrial exhibition taking place there.

During this trip to England and France, Werner came to the conclusion that, in the long run, there was no money to be made in minor unsystematic inventions. The result, eventually, was the founding of Siemens & Halske. Since his financial means were soon exhausted, Werner, after his return to Berlin, again took up serious studies in physics, established contacts with other researchers, and became more and more interested in electrical experiments. During this period he also involved himself in experiments with electrical telegraphy, concentrating on improving the magnetic pointer telegraph invented by Wheatstone. Meanwhile Werner conducted an intensive correspondence with his brother Wilhelm, supporting his work with numerous suggestions and comments. In his electrical experiments, Werner worked together with several "practical craftsmen," first with the clockmaker Ferdinand Leonhardt, with whom he built his first devices for electrical telegraphy. Werner turned to the master mechanic Johann Georg Halske for the implementation of his pioneering advancements in the field of telegraphy, improvements on Wheatstone's pointer telegraph. Together with his partner Johann Friedrich Bötticher, Halske ran the mechanical establishment Bötticher & Halske, which produced precision equipment. Werner succeeded in winning Halske's total and enthusiastic support for his projects. In the autumn of 1847 Werner even managed to persuade Halske to close down his previous business and to join him in founding a new venture, the Telegraph System Construction Enterprise Siemens & Halske (Telegraphen-Bauanstalt Siemens & Halske).

Siemens and Halske began to live together in a house, on the ground floor of which was located the workshop of the new enterprise. Since Werner at that time had next to no equity capital at his disposal, his cousin, the legal official Johann Georg Siemens, bought an interest in the firm of 6,842 thalers—somewhat more than 20,000 marks—in exchange for a share in the profits over a period of six years. On October 12, 1847, the workshop, employing ten workmen, was opened in a rear building at 19 Schöneberger Straße in Berlin. Of the profits, Werner Siemens and Georg Halske were each supposed to receive two-fifths of the total, and Georg Siemens one-fifth.

To meet his obligations to support his younger brothers and sisters, and to avoid being regarded as a "deserter" in the unstable political period prior to the March revolution in 1848, Werner stayed in the military service for the time being and devoted himself to his new enterprise in his spare time. The fact of his being, by virtue of his army position, a consultant member of the Prussian Telegraph Commission turned out to be a particularly favorable coincidence. Werner's medium-term plans, however, were to devote himself completely to the telegraph business and to his firm. In a lecture in 1879 Werner von Siemens, looking back, summed up his impressions on the development of electrical telegraphy:

> Soon after Volta, for the design of the column named after
> him, had discovered a way to produce a continuous electric
> current, Dr. Soemmerring in 1808 suggested using the current

The first Siemens & Halske workshop, 19 Schöneberger Straße, Berlin, 1847–1952

for telegraphic means. It took quite some time of serious research work, however, before his idea could be materialized in practice. Only after the discovery of the effects of electric current across some distance by Ørsted, and after the laws governing the use of electricity had been uncovered by men such as Ampère, Arago, Faraday, Gauss, Weber, Wheatstone and many more, did the implementation of Soemmerring's audacious plan finally become feasible. But while the telegraphs, constructed at the beginning of the thirties by Gauss and Weber in Göttingen and by Steinheil near Munich, operated well, another decade passed before the pragmatic approach of the Americans and English actually started practical telegraphy. From that time on, in the middle of the forties, telegraphy began to develop and expand rapidly. . . . All nations participated in this race, with our German fatherland being one of the foremost competitors.[8]

Germany's position among the leaders was, in no small measure, due to Werner von Siemens. The first telegraph he had built was a modification of an English instrument developed by Wheatstone, which was soon replaced by a design by Samuel Morse, which from then on served as a prototype and was continuously improved.

The Influence of the Political Situation on Siemens's Business Activities

The early years of Werner von Siemens's business activities were deeply influenced by the political conditions of the time. Contrary to the hopes of the liberal middle classes, the accession of King Friedrich Wilhelm IV in 1840 did not result in a reversal of the Prussian "Politics of Restoration" of the 1830s. After 1846 the disappointment over the failure of Prussia to develop a constitutional state was intensified by a rapidly accelerating economic recession. Poor harvests caused real famines in large sectors of the population. In this strained political and economic situation, the February revolution of 1848 in Paris triggered the March revolution in Berlin.

The Siemens brothers were among the most vigorous supporters of the revolution, whose aims completely matched the
national and liberal ideas that, according to Werner, had
molded their education.[9] Wilhelm expressed this viewpoint
most clearly; living in England, he could adopt an especially
radical-liberal attitude. As he wrote to Werner:

> F.W. [Friedrich Wilhelm], by the way, is a king who suits me
> well; he does his utmost to teach you how unsatisfactory his
> present government is, and by his opposition he also offers
> the advantage that the people can win liberty by their own
> struggle. Let us hope that in his answer to the different politi-
> cians, he will claim to have more wits in his big toe than is to
> be found in the heads of all the parliamentarians put together
> and that, for this very reason, he is unable to attach any great
> importance to their resolutions. . . . Our typical "German
> Michel" will probably get his liberty in the end and will swear
> by his nightcap that he will never let others make an ass of
> him again. Metternich, with his legions of clerics, customs
> officers, privy councillors, censors, diplomats, and bureau-
> crats requiring permits for everything, will go to hell and will
> so preoccupy the devil that he will never again lead any Ger-
> man astray. Sabers and cannons will also be unnecessary in
> the future.[10]

As a Prussian officer Werner had to be more restrained in
his comments, but as a consequence of his political opinions he
had to put up with the possibility of setbacks in his career. In
1845 he cosigned a declaration in support of Johannes Ronge
and directed against the "shady obscurantists" ("Dunkelmän-
ner"). He narrowly escaped reassignment as a reprimand by
the military authorities only by developing a new kind of gun
cotton, the report on which he dispatched directly to the secretary of the army. In his letters to Wilhelm he commented em-
phatically on the revolution everybody was longing for. Even
before March 18 he wrote under the spell of the events in
France: "Vive la France! I would shout together with you from
the bottom of my heart, if one still had the luck to belong morally to the proletarian class! Yet this does not matter much; we

are making great progress. Such a commotion of minds, such an urge to throw off all the unworthy fetters and barriers, must come to fruition!"[11] And only a few days later Werner gave a report from revolutionary Berlin: "I hurry, dear brother, to send you the first salute from a *free country!*"[12]

For the business activities of the Telegraph System Construction Enterprise, however, the revolution, so enthusiastically welcomed by Werner, meant a severe setback at first. The Telegraph Commission discontinued all activities for the time being, yet without being formally dissolved.

On the other hand, events associated with the revolution allowed Werner to follow his national sentiments in his military career. In January 1848 Denmark had attempted to integrate Schleswig, which was a Danish feudal territory but was also joined in a real union with Holstein, which belonged to Germany, into the Danish nation. Both duchies, Schleswig and Holstein, took part in the revolution and tried to break their ties to Denmark and join the German Confederation. This was a constitutionally controversial situation, since in Schleswig the revolutionaries had risen against their legitimate prince. Prussia and other members of the German Confederation, commissioned by the Confederation with the conduct of war against the Danes, at first hesitated to begin an armed intervention. Werner von Siemens, acting without any official order, in April 1848 set off for Kiel, where his sister Mathilde and her husband, Professor Himly, had moved. On his own initiative, supported by his brother-in-law, Werner developed underwater mines with electrical fuses, which were employed with great success in protecting the harbor of Kiel against Danish warships.

By the time Werner received an official order from the Prussian authorities for the defense of the harbor of Eckernförde and had even been appointed commander of Friedrichsort, he had already lost interest in this adventurous diversion into warfare and immediately returned to Berlin. In his memoirs he writes in great detail and with evident pleasure about this adventure, which militarily—even if not politically—had had a victorious outcome for Prussia.

Carl Siemens, ca. 1860

Since Wilhelm had taken up permanent residence in England, two of the younger brothers, Carl and Friedrich, had become old enough that the question of their future education, training, and professional life had arisen. After Wilhelm had succeeded in selling the gold-plating patent in England, Friedrich, Carl, and Walter had lived with Werner in Berlin and had attended school there. Before that time they had lived with their uncle in Lübeck. After leaving school, Friedrich first had the intention of going to sea, but a short probationary period revealed that he was not physically fit enough for the hard life involved. His two elder brothers therefore tried to find him a suitable place as an apprentice. When Friedrich began this mechanical training in autumn 1847 he insisted that the option of joining his brother Wilhelm in England be kept open.

At first Carl also had it in mind to go to sea. Werner succeeded, however, in directing his interests more to chemistry and physics. In 1846 Carl left school in the ninth grade and started work as a chemist with the Berlin firm Haslinger & Schondorf.

All the brothers remained very close. After the March revolution both Carl and Friedrich followed Werner to Kiel, and from there Friedrich traveled to England for the first time, to work on Werner's telegraph projects. Working as an assistant to his brother-in-law, Professor Himly, Carl stayed in Kiel a while longer. This arrangement did not meet with the approval of his brothers at all. They were of the opinion that in Kiel Carl would probably cultivate his "phlegmatic nature" too much. The news of the discovery of gold in California led the two younger brothers, Friedrich and Carl, to consider emigrating to the United States. Werner expressed a willingness to assist them but asked them to reconsider their decision before departing, and they decided to stay in Europe.

Their decision not to emigrate probably meant that Carl and Friedrich enjoyed more good fortune than most of the men who rushed to California dreaming of quick fortunes in the gold mines. Favorable developments in the second half of 1848 and in following years opened up new and expanded business activities for all four of the brothers. They obtained contracts for the construction of telegraph lines in Germany between Berlin and Cologne and between Berlin and Frankfurt. Siemens & Halske fulfilled these contracts with great success within a few months, which allowed Werner in the autumn of 1849 to quit the army after twelve years of service. His physical and mental abilities were now fully required by the Telegraph System Construction Enterprise. Moreover, while for a time as a military officer Werner had been able to exert influence on the promotion of telegraphy, civilian uses of the telegraph had now become the growth area for the new technology. This situation was reflected in the transfer of the responsibility for telegraphy from the Prussian War Department to the Ministry for Trade and Commerce. Werner was glad to hand in his papers. His military service had provided him with training in engineering and allowed him time for his inventions and scientific experiments. Nor had his liberal political attitude done him any harm. Therefore, in his memoirs he expressed a pleasant memory of his military service in general. He mentioned that the strict hierarchical military order—which, by the way, was dominant in the Prussian civilian authorities as well—was always alleviated somewhat by the "spirit of camaraderie." All in all, however, we are left with the impression that now Werner was finally able to make full use of his skills as a free businessman.

Meanwhile, Wilhelm Siemens was becoming more successful in England. In 1849 he found regular work with the mechanical engineering company Fox & Henderson in Birmingham. They guaranteed him flexible working hours, promised him a share in the benefits from patents, and paid him a fixed annual salary. With this money Wilhelm was able to improve his precarious economic situation, which for years, apart from occasional small profits drawn from patent licenses, had kept him dependent on the financial support of his brother.

The status and security of the two elder brothers gave them an opportunity to allow the younger brothers a greater share in the joint business. With these prospects, the two soon gave up their plans for emigration to the United States. Wilhelm was able to win a permanent job for Friedrich also with Fox & Henderson. Carl, for the time being, entered Siemens & Halske in Berlin and worked as a designer of telegraph lines.

3

The Founding of the Enterprise and the First Period of Expansion: 1840s to Mid-1860s

The Development of the Telegraph Network

In addition to the initiation and expansion of railway lines and the changes in heavy industry, the development of communication technology was one of the characteristic features of the period of industrialization. Telegraphy, bridging long distances at high speed, created a base for the increasing international business relations and, eventually, the global economy. After experiments in the field of optical telegraphy, which turned out to be unreliable (inoperative during fog or at night) and not suitable for long-distance service, in the 1840s the first usable electric telegraphs were constructed on the basis of the instruments invented by Samuel Soemmerring (in 1809) and Samuel Morse (in 1837). The first long-distance telegraph went into operation in 1844 between Washington, D.C., and Baltimore, Maryland, in the United States.[1]

Werner von Siemens made important improvements to early telegraph technology. In 1846 he succeeded in improving the Wheatstone pointer type telegraph, which was used in England. While these improvements were soon surpassed by the

45

The Atlantic cable being covered with gutta-percha

Morse telegraphs, Siemens's developments came in time to help him achieve his first successes in supplying the Prussian state telegraphs. With the help of his brother Wilhelm, he was also introduced to the technique of insulating electrical conductors by means of gutta-percha (natural latex). In 1846 Wilhelm sent him a sample of this insulating material, which the English physician Montgomery had brought home from Singapore in 1842. To insulate wires with gutta-percha, Werner in 1847 constructed a press permitting the application of a seamless insulating coat on a wire.[2] The discovery of gutta-percha, a thickened sap with thermoplastic properties obtained from the gutta-percha tree, was a fortunate stroke of luck, for gutta-percha provided an excellent insulating material for underground cables. Werner's development of the gutta-percha press allowed his firm to begin modern-style telecommunications, doing so even when batteries composed of galvanic elements were still the only source available for the required electrical energy.

The pointer telegraph devised by Werner von Siemens represented a fundamentally new solution to the problem of electrical transmission of information. The transmitter and the receiver were identically designed. A battery to provide power and a line consisting of one insulated conductor for the forward and one for the return connection between the two stations were also required. During operation a self-interrupting mechanism invented by Wagner and Neef (and still used in doorbells) chopped the direct current supplied by the battery into a train of equal pulses. As these pulses traveled in a closed loop from the battery and the transmitter through the line to the receiver and through the other line back to the battery, the incremental pointer systems of the transmitter and of the receiver rotated in step to the beat of the pulses during transmission of the message. The letters of the alphabet and a few special symbols were assigned to thirty radially arranged keys at the top of the telegraph. As soon as a key at the transmitting station was depressed, the pointers of the transmitting telegraph and of the receiving telegraph started to turn simultaneously to the respective key, indicating the letter of the depressed key at the transmitting station to the operator at the receiving station. For each letter to be transmitted, the pointers always had to travel the full circle of thirty positions, first to the position of the depressed key, and then in the same direction of rotation back to the initial position. This took up a lot of time, and there was also the need to write down each letter indicated at the receiver before the next letter of the message could be accepted.

The American Morse telegraphs, transmitting in code and printing a maximum of five dots and/or dashes per character on a ribbon of paper, operated at a higher speed—about a hundred characters per minute compared to forty characters for the pointer telegraph—and soon became more popular. Morse code lowered the costs for the transmission of information, since more telegrams could be sent per unit of time. While admittedly Morse telegraphs required specially trained operators, the details of operation and the Morse code were easy to learn. Since they were simpler to operate, however, and required only a short instruction period, the pointer telegraphs were still used by railway companies for many more years.

Werner immediately tried to commercialize his inventions. After he had been granted patents in England and France, the basis for his business activities had been established. In most countries the organization of the telegraph networks was governed by the interests of the military authorities, which were eager to have a simple and rapid means of communication. Accordingly, most of the European states first implemented a state telegraph network. With increasing civilian utilization of the telegraph—which soon became of vital importance for the stock exchanges, for example—private operating companies were also founded. Railway administrations constituted another expanding group of customers. The strong concentration of the demand for telegraphs among governments and a few private operators demonstrated very early the specific market structure for telegraphs.[3]

The special structure of the telegraph industry gave Siemens & Halske an unusual business opportunity. Because of the concentrated demand, fiscal and sometimes prestige-oriented considerations had a substantial influence on the emerging telegraph industry. The development of the telegraph industry was, to a large extent, separate from the general economic situation, and the firms in the industry accordingly had to develop special marketing strategies. Among these essential efforts were the cultivation of personal contacts with the respective national telegraph authorities of target states, and also the early establishment of overseas contacts to ensure a sufficient backlog of orders for a reasonable amount of time. Despite its great importance for the improvement of the infrastructure, the telegraph industry was generally not a significant factor in the overall economy. Thus, unlike railway construction, it played hardly any role in the labor market as an employer or in the demand for raw materials. This structural environment has to be taken into account in evaluating the entrepreneurial activities of Werner von Siemens and his brothers.

The Beginnings of the Telegraph System Construction Enterprise

Werner von Siemens founded his first establishment, the Telegraph System Construction Enterprise Siemens & Halske, without any capital of his own. As we have seen in the previous chapter, his partners were the master mechanic Johann Georg Halske, who had already assisted him during the development of the pointer telegraph, and his cousin, the judicial officer Johann Georg Siemens. Werner von Siemens put his patents at the disposal of the new enterprise; Halske, who had already, together with a partner, run a workshop of his own, contributed his practical experience both in craftsmanship and in organizing a workshop.

This division of management in Siemens & Halske proved advantageous. Halske pledged to place all his efforts into the operation of the workshop, while Werner, for the time being, remained in the military service. Werner thus was able to make profitable use of his position in the Telegraph Commission for winning orders, a task that was—as were all external affairs and the representation of the firm—within Werner's planned scope of activities. Meanwhile, as the supplier of capital, the cousin, Johann Georg Siemens, pledged to invest the sum of 10,000 thalers in three annual installments, from 1846 to 1848. Because of the failed revolution of March 1848, however, the last installment was never paid. The partnership contract stipulated a proportional sharing of the future profits: Werner von Siemens and Georg Halske were to get two-fifths each, while the "capitalist" Georg Siemens was to get one-fifth. Werner was also to receive one-third of the royalties for his patents sold abroad.

The rapid founding of an entrepreneurial firm without an elaborate formal bureaucracy and its financing with the help of wealthy relatives were typical phenomena in the early period of German industrialization. The founding of the Telegraph System Construction Enterprise at a time of financial and political crisis was less typical, however. The successful establishment of a new enterprise in a situation of such political and economic uncertainty clearly showed that the newly developing telegraph industry was largely able to operate independently of general economic conditions. Furthermore, the predominantly manual production of telegraphs did not require a large capital appropriation. All telegraphs were produced individually by skilled workers, and large machines were unnecessary. Siemens & Halske did not introduce its first steam engine to provide mechanical power for the wholesale production of standardized parts until 1863.[4]

This large degree of independence from the overall economic situation signified, on the other hand, a dependence on only a few customers: the military, somewhat later the state telegraph system, and the railways. With regard to the Telegraph System Construction Enterprise, this disadvantage was compensated for by the company's almost complete monopoly as the supplier of such devices and by the outstanding personal contacts Werner von Siemens had established. Even before founding the firm, he had entered into promising negotiations with the Prussian Telegraph Commission, the Anhalt railway authorities in Germany, and the ambassador of Russia. By the time the firm was established, it could already count on some almost solid contracts. Accordingly, the financial risk was comparatively low.

Following a competitive bid, which owing to the revolution in the spring did not take place until August 1848, Werner von Siemens won the contract for the construction of a telegraph line between Berlin and Frankfurt am Main. This line was not to make use of his pointer telegraphs, however, but the improved Morse telegraphs. A few months later this line was used on March 28, 1849, to transmit the news of the election of the Prussian king Friedrich Wilhelm IV as German hereditary emperor from St. Paul's Church, the makeshift seat of the preliminary parliament in Frankfurt, to Berlin. The success of the line meant that Siemens & Halske was in business for good.

In reaction to this first great success, Werner von Siemens, who in 1848 had still considered transferring into the Prussian civil service in hopes of becoming inspector general of the

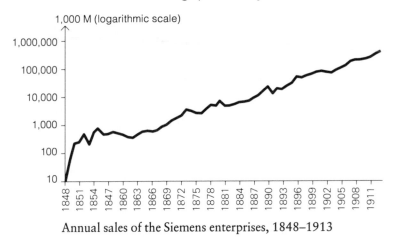

1,000 M (logarithmic scale)

Annual sales of the Siemens enterprises, 1848–1913

Prussian telegraph system, now decided to resign his commission as an army officer and devote himself fully to his enterprise. His friend and fellow student William Meyer became his successor as the technical director of the Telegraph Commission. Their friendship continued, and Meyer later held power of attorney and was a senior engineer for Siemens & Halske.

The close ties with the Prussian telegraph authorities did not last long, though. During the summer of 1849, when Werner was engaged with the construction of new lines in the Prussian Rhineland provinces, the first difficulties arose. The faulty insulation of underground lines had caused considerable trouble in the telegraph network. Werner von Siemens tried to justify himself by stating that he had been forced to use the cheapest methods. The principal deficiency was probably due to the addition of sulfur to the gutta-percha before insulating the electrical conductors: the sulfur gradually reacted with the copper conductors, turning them into crumbling copper sulfide. The result was shunt connections, cross-interference, and errors in the printing of the dots and dashes of the Morse code. To make matters worse, the work on the Frankfurt-Berlin line had been carried out "somewhat hastily" because of the political circumstances.[5] Such troubles and disturbances kept arising, and in 1851 the Prussian telegraph authorities broke off business relations with Siemens & Halske. The director of the Telegraph Commission, Friedrich Wilhelm Nottebohm, revoked all follow-up orders for Siemens & Halske, plunging the young enterprise into its first serious crisis.[6] Although in 1851 the firm won an important contract for the Berlin-Hamburg railway amounting to 32,000 thalers, it was obvious that, after the cancellation of the orders by the Prussian authorities, long-term economic survival would depend on developing a flourishing business abroad.

The Nottebohm crisis highlights two specific problems of the young telegraph business: (1) A product and a system had to be manufactured and installed before it was technically fully developed. Competition therefore took place primarily on the level of technical standards, not prices. (2) The dependence of the business on a few customers and the problem of competently evaluating technical standards led to biased decisions in the awarding of contracts. Because the different technical standards of the products could not be compared on the basis of price, in the long run the awarding of contracts was decided by

Tally of business results for Siemens & Halske, October 1847 through January 1, 1850

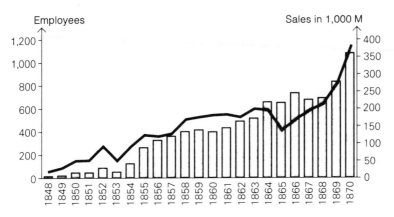

Employees (line) and sales (columns) of Siemens & Halske, 1848–1870

personal acquaintances, sympathies and aversions, or the general "reputation" of a firm. The Nottebohm crisis demonstrated how decisions based on personality and reputation were easily reversible, and the reversal could grievously wound a previously successful enterprise.

Similarly, Siemens & Halske had no experience in calculating costs and capacity. In the face of large orders, the firm could hardly keep up with the production of telegraphs and accessories, while between construction contracts, work shortages and periods of underemployment repeatedly endangered the survival of the firm. This fundamental problem was impossible to solve as long as the enterprise was engaged exclusively or at least chiefly in the telegraph business. Siemens & Halske tried to counteract this situation by means of early diversification. The Berlin plant, for example, switched to the production of water meters for the English market after the falloff in Russian telegraph orders at the end of the 1850s. These meters had been developed on the initiative of Wilhelm Siemens, who had taken out a patent for them.[7] Although manufacturing the water meters was barely profitable for several years, this branch of production allowed Siemens & Halske to keep and employ a permanent body of skilled workers even at times of few orders in other fields.[8] In Berlin, for instance, after the first expansion up to the middle of the 1860s, about 150 workers were employed almost continuously, with only a few (9 in 1867) being unskilled workers.[9]

Orders for telegraphs from abroad could not compensate for such fluctuations, typical of the telegraph business, since the same problems existed abroad as in Prussia. Thus the Nottebohm crisis itself was not the cause of the strong international involvement of the firm. From the start of the enterprise, Werner, on his own initiative and also through his brother Wilhelm, had endeavored to establish international contacts. Nonetheless, the withdrawal of all Prussian orders after 1851 increased the necessity to succeed abroad for the sake of the economic survival of the enterprise.

Foreign ventures were not always successful, however. Siemens & Halske enjoyed early profits in Russia and England but experienced failure in Belgium and France. As in Prussia, Werner had in France and Belgium attempted to gain access to the market via scientific institutions. In February of 1850 he visited Brussels, spent a short time with Wilhelm in London, and then visited Paris in April. There he had the opportunity to establish private contacts, to give a lecture at the Academy on his inventions and innovations in the field of telegraphy, and to have this lecture published in the *Journal de physique et chimie* a few weeks later. Although Werner was very happy about this scientific success and had high hopes for orders from France, they did not materialize.[10] The cause of this lack of success in France lay in the increasingly strained political relations between France and Germany after 1840, which reached their climax in the war of 1870–71, followed by a period of cool relations and open resentment.[11] This experience proved that a good reputation in scientific and technical fields was not always sufficient to establish permanent business relations.

Generally speaking, in marketing, Siemens & Halske pursued personal contacts and scientific discussions. Because of the company's narrow financial base and the novelty of its products, a different approach is hard to imagine. In consequence, cultivation of business relations was left almost entirely to Werner von Siemens personally and could at most be delegated to his equally expert brothers Wilhelm, Friedrich, and Carl.

One of the most effective publicity efforts of the young enterprise—particularly during the Nottebohm crisis—was its participation in the Crystal Palace Exhibition, the first world exposition, which took place in London in 1851. In order to help Wilhelm and Friedrich Siemens, who were both employed at a firm in Birmingham and could take only temporary time off, Carl traveled to London in the spring of 1851 to represent Siemens & Halske at the exposition. Wilhelm participated very little in the demonstration of Siemens products during the exhibition, but he worked hard to establish business contacts, entering into direct negotiations with American companies and with the East India Company. At first these efforts came to nothing, although the enterprise Siemens & Halske did gain some international publicity, enhanced by winning the Council Medal, a mark of high distinction awarded by the organizers of the exposition.

Shortly after the successful exposition in England, Carl Siemens tried to expand the business into France, but again Siemens & Halske was without success there. On Werner's behalf, Carl was supposed to establish a subsidiary in Paris and not be content with just an agency. This company, founded hastily without considering the potential for sales, had to be closed in December 1852. Carl, aged twenty-three at the time, left France with the conclusion, "Lots of money spent, nothing gained and, additionally, a miserable life during that period of time."[12] Werner encouraged Carl not to be disappointed, yet he supported an immediate retreat in the face of the disastrous results.[13]

First Orders from Russia and Subsequent Expansion in the East

New business with Russia after 1850 initiated a boom period for Siemens & Halske. Thanks to long-term maintenance contracts, this business assured continuous earnings into the 1860s. Reflecting back on his life and career, Werner rated the establishment of these business connections as a decisive break: "The year 1852 represented a decisive turning point in my personal as well as in my business life."[14] The personal turning point was his engagement and later marriage to Mathilde Drumann, the daughter of a professor from Königsberg in eastern Prussia. The business turning point, of course, was connected with the development in Russia.

As we have seen, Werner had conducted exploratory talks with the Russian ambassador in Berlin even before the founding of Siemens & Halske. For the time being, however, he had discontinued these talks, not least because of political doubts about "reactionary" Russia. As late as 1848, Werner was still complaining to his brothers Friedrich and Wilhelm about the resurrection of conservative forces: "I do not wish to support this trend, far less stand on Russia's side! . . . Prussianism is rising to power again quite blatantly. This trend is reinforced by the unpolitical stance of the Frankfurt leftists, insulting Prussia's pride." At the same time, he emphasized that in all probability, as a result of developments so far, Germany would become more or less Prussian, and he conceded, "My private interest is right now quite favorably inclined toward the latter."[15] Owing to the Nottebohm crisis, the opportunities opening up in Russia were most welcome for Werner von Siemens and his young enterprise, causing him to finally drop his political objections. Still, he repeatedly expressed indignation over the despotic methods of the Russian national telegraph administration.

At the beginning of the 1850s Russia offered a very promising market for telegraphy. The inadequate infrastructure of the vast empire made a fundamental improvement in communications mandatory, for political, military, and economic reasons. Accordingly, the interest in the new technology shown in influential political and military circles, and also by Czar Nicholas I personally, was great. Even though systematic industrialization of the country did not begin until the end of the nineteenth century, at an early stage the czarist government turned its attention toward completion of the infrastructure—including both railroads and telegraphs. In 1852 the first important railroad line, between St. Petersburg and Moscow, was completed, creating the first opportunity for a telegraph company in the empire. Russia herself had no technically skilled workers at her disposal and was therefore dependent on supplies from abroad for the manufacture, installation, and maintenance of both railroad and telegraph lines.

The first contacts between Werner von Siemens and the Russian government began as early as 1847. Further negotiations with the Russian ambassador in Berlin followed in 1849, and in 1851 Siemens & Halske received a first order for seventy-five pointer telegraphs for the St. Petersburg–Moscow railroad line. As was the case with the railroads, the contract for the construction of pointer telegraphs resulted from the recommendation of engineers who had traveled to western Europe; it was not awarded on the basis of competitive bidding by invited firms. Werner von Siemens had always recognized the importance of personal contacts, such as he had maintained with the Russian ambassador, Karl von Lüders. With this in mind, he decided to travel to Russia for the first time at the beginning of 1852. Two more visits to St. Petersburg, one in the same year and the other at the beginning of 1853, were to follow. During these stays in Russia, Werner appointed a Mr. Kapherr, a merchant of German extraction from St. Petersburg, as the representative for Siemens & Halske. He also succeeded in establishing direct contacts with the head of the Russian national telegraphy, Count Kleinmichel, the person who decided the awarding of contracts. Werner's ability to quickly adapt to the local Russian customs—for example, the handing out of generous gifts to leading officials—facilitated his access to orders.

Siemens & Halske was soon to benefit from its contacts in Russia. Werner von Siemens, during his second visit in 1852, induced Count Kleinmichel to award Siemens & Halske the contract for the construction of the telegraph lines between St. Petersburg and Moscow. Soon, in 1853, a second contract followed, to construct a telegraph line from St. Petersburg to Kronstadt through Oranienbaum. This made it necessary to send a permanent representative of the firm to St. Petersburg. Mr. Kapherr was not qualified for such an assignment, nor had he won the full confidence of the top management of

Siemens & Halske. Werner decided to send his brother Carl, who after the failed attempt to found a subsidiary in Paris was again at the firm's disposal, to St. Petersburg. Again, kinship ties proved essential for the continued expansion of Siemens & Halske in a desirable foreign market. Carl traveled first to Warsaw, since Halske at the same time had succeeded in securing an order from the Russian governor-general for Poland for the construction of a telegraph line from Warsaw to the German border. Shortly afterward Carl moved to St. Petersburg.

The Russian assignment was not an easy one for Carl Siemens. Because of his youth, Carl at first had difficulty commanding respect in St. Petersburg. Count Kleinmichel even seemed to be somewhat annoyed that Werner had sent him a young man just twenty-four years of age to be in charge of the construction project. However, Carl's ability to work out solutions to problems in a rapid and competent fashion quickly convinced Kleinmichel that Werner had made a wise choice, and soon a particularly good relationship developed between the two men. Carl also earned the full respect of his older brother. As early as November 1853 Carl was granted full power of attorney for the Russian business of Siemens & Halske and was from that time on authorized to conclude contracts for the Berlin enterprise.

The outbreak of the Crimean War between Russia and Turkey in November 1853 turned out to be particularly profitable for the development of the business. In March 1854 England joined Turkish forces in order to protect her position in the Black Sea and the narrows at the Bosporus. In Berlin the management of Siemens & Halske was initially worried about the attitude of the Prussian government—in March 1854 business deals at a volume of 350,000 rubles were pending—but the central powers in Europe, indecisive, observed a strict neutrality throughout the war. The only negative impact of the war was a delay in the shipment of English maritime telegraph cables made by the English firm Newall & Co. to Russia for the line to Kronstadt. This delay caused Carl, who was in fear of an English embargo, some disquieting weeks. With this exception, the war created a good flow of orders. The Russian

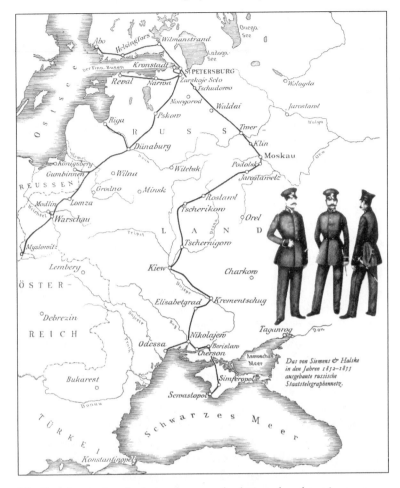

The Russian national telegraph network, designed and put in operation by Siemens & Halske between 1852 and 1855

military authorities were particularly interested in a telegraph line to the Crimea, in order to establish a permanent connection to the fortress of Sebastopol, which was besieged beginning in September of 1854. Consequently, Siemens & Halske received an order for the construction of a telegraph line connecting Moscow and Sebastopol via Kiev.

Encouraged by the increasing importance of the business in Russia, as early as the summer of 1854 Werner began to think of reorganizing the relationship between St. Petersburg and Berlin. The immediate cause of the reconfiguration was the desire of Johann Georg Siemens to retire from the firm as a partner. Georg Siemens was paid the very large sum of 50,000 thalers in five annual installments. The result was a semiautonomous business in Russia under the direction of Carl Siemens. Carl took his cousin Georg's place and was allocated a share in the company equivalent to one-fifth of the firm's capital. Thus his previous efforts were acknowledged, since under his management business in Russia had made the largest contribution to the firm's overall profit. The arrangement between Carl and Siemens & Halske was a twelve-year contract (beginning January 1, 1855), after the expiration of which Carl would have the option of going into business in Russia for himself.[16] Although this contract defined the firm in St. Petersburg as a branch of the parent company in Berlin, in effect Carl ran the Russian business independently, with its own capital and its own profit accounts. A supplementary agreement of October 1, 1855, added to the business contract of January 1, affirmed this status by a formal contract.[17]

As the Russian business progressed favorably, the military importance of the commissions and the course of the war interfered with the work to be performed by Siemens & Halske. The Russian government tried to bring all kinds of pressure to bear upon Siemens & Halske to assure a rapid completion of the lines. During a visit in 1855 Werner von Siemens was initially refused permission to leave the country until the line between Odessa and Sebastopol was completed. This intervention had no noticeable effect on the completion of the telegraph line to the Crimean peninsula. The Crimean line finally became operational in September 1855, only to transmit the news of the surrender of the fortress of Sebastopol.

With the end of the Crimean War, the wartime boom experienced by Siemens & Halske also fizzled. Because of its weak financial position, the Russian government awarded no new orders for the construction of telegraph lines after 1856. After the death of Czar Nicholas I, moreover, his successor, Alexander II, removed Count Kleinmichel from his position as director of the national state telegraphy—an even more disastrous event for Siemens's telegraph business, since Carl now lost his direct personal access to the man in charge of awarding contracts. The representative of Siemens & Halske in St. Petersburg, Mr. Kapherr, who in the meantime had become Carl's father-in-law, was not on good terms with Kleinmichel's successor. Moreover, problems increasingly arose in the business relations between Carl Siemens and Kapherr, despite Carl's marriage to his daughter Marie, probably because after Carl had independently taken over the St. Petersburg business, no clear demarcation of the respective responsibilities of the two men had been defined.

Despite these unfavorable developments, Siemens and Halske's opportunities for making money in Russia were still good, because in 1855 maintenance contracts for a period of twelve years had been signed for the lines constructed by the firm. For this so-called remount (Russ. *remont,* "repairs, maintenance") the Russian subsidiary operated a small workshop in St. Petersburg and engineering offices in St. Petersburg, Kiev, and Odessa, each of which was in charge of monitoring and servicing the telegraph lines in a specific area. Because of the generally low level of technical competence of other firms, Siemens & Halske did not have to fear competition or a premature revocation of the contracts. As the costs for the maintenance services had first appeared to be very difficult to estimate, Siemens & Halske had specified high maintenance fees and placed two-thirds of the earnings in a "remount" reserve fund to cover eventual cost overruns. In the meantime, another invention by Werner von Siemens, the so-called Tartar galvanometer, soon allowed the precise location of faults. This device reduced the personnel requirements for maintenance work to a minimum, as repair teams were now able to respond rapidly and right on target. Thus, the "remount" earnings turned out to be a lucrative source of revenue, even though estimates on the exact magnitude of the profits differ slightly. (The conservative calculations by Kirchner, however, also arrive at a total profit of 1.6 million rubles.)[18]

The Business Results of the "Remount" (in rubles)

Year	Expenditures	Revenue	Profit
1856	400,863	460,994	60,310
1857	325,450	423,645	98,194
1858	332,789	142,415	79,625
1859	388,225	511,727	123,502
1860	533,891	688,533	152,662
1861	318,802	443,385	124,582
1862	238,500	343,191	104,691
1863	323,904	419,364	95,460
1864	191,060	279,155	88,094
1865	171,771	269,751	97,979

From 1853 until 1855 the Russian business guaranteed the utilization of the full capacity of the facilities of the parent company in Berlin. After that time, the maintenance work dropped to a volume just sufficient to keep the workshop in St. Petersburg busy. Some small additional business with Russia other than the telegraphy branch developed promisingly, however. For example, Werner had developed an instrument to determine the percentage of alcohol present in a liquid, which was widely employed by the Russian tax authorities in the taxation of alcohol.

Even after the end of the Crimean War, the extensive construction of telegraph lines and the maintenance contracts assured Siemens & Halske a favorable reputation in Russia. Werner von Siemens was very pleased when the firm received the title of "Contract Partners for the Construction and the Maintenance of the Imperial Russian Telegraph Lines" and was given the right to have their officials wear uniforms, a measure that greatly added to their authority and the respect in which they were held.[19] Even after expiration of the contracts in 1867, Siemens was able to hold its ground successfully against strong competition from abroad and to keep on selling telegraphs and safety systems for the Russian railways. The equipment for lighting engineering developed by Siemens & Halske in the 1880s also rapidly found an open and important market in Russia.

The extensive export business with Russia necessitated some reforms in the organizational structure of the parent firm in Berlin; such reforms, however, were kept to a minimum as far as possible. The company hired a full-time accountant in 1855, Carl Haase, who continued in the position for many years. For additional support, William Meyer received power of attorney in the same year and was put in charge primarily of the organization and made a supervisor of executive personnel. The delays in the transfer of payments between Berlin and St. Petersburg made it necessary to resort to banks for temporary financing to bypass bottlenecks resulting from the time lapse between payments received and the financial obligations of the enterprise to suppliers and subcontractors. As a general rule, the Russian government made the payments to Kapherr, who then arranged the issue of bills of exchange payable at major places in Germany. These bills of exchange were then redeemed by the banker Magnus in Berlin. Kapherr's financial services cost the firm dearly, because he claimed a commission of 10% for all business transactions.

There was a turning point for the business in Russia in 1867, for two reasons. First, the maintenance contracts with the Russian government, which had been quite profitable for Siemens & Halske, expired. Second, Carl Siemens left St. Petersburg for health reasons, settling first in Tbilisi and later in London. The true reason for his disengagement, however, was probably not concern for his health but rather dismay over the doldrums afflicting the St. Petersburg branch of Siemens & Halske, making the thought of continuing his activities in the Russian capital not very attractive. One result of the lower volume of business was changes in the organization. Because of the original contract with Halske, the Russian enterprise, which had been independent, was placed into liquidation to allow determination of the share of the assets due to Halske. In the course of the reorganization of the whole setup, the Russian enterprise was converted into a branch of the parent company in Berlin.

Carl Siemens's departure from Russia proved temporary (he was uncomfortable being under the shadow of his elder brother Wilhelm), and his return brought further changes in business there. Profits during the 1870s were not especially good, but Carl eventually succeeded in reversing the firm's fortunes in Russia. He reestablished the relationship between St. Petersburg and Berlin to its pre-1868 status: Siemens & Halske in St. Petersburg became a subsidiary of the parent company, authorized for independent accounting.

Immediately after his return, Carl began to liquidate a china factory in Gorodok, established in 1861, which had caused heavy losses. Carl had initially built it as a glass factory, after buying the Chmelewo estate at Lake Ilmen for 60,000 rubles, in order to field-test the regenerative process for the heating of industrial furnaces invented by his brother Friedrich.[20] As Carl himself was no expert in the production of glass, he had to rely almost totally on the master foreman of the works and, later, on the technical directors of the firm. This condition soon turned into a serious handicap. To make matters worse, there was also a slump in prices from 1861 to 1864, from 60–65 rubles per box of glass down to 45 rubles. Accordingly, the glass factory turned into the "rotten apple" of the business in Russia.[21] An attempt by Carl to convert the facility into a factory for china proved to be a misjudgment. In 1881 Werner von Siemens stated: "It was unfortunate not to have stuck to the latter (the glass factory). With the enormous improvements in glass production developed by Fritz and under his supervision, the production of bottles might most likely have turned out a useful result."[22]

Initially, the china factory produced insulators to meet the firm's own demands; it also made crockery to fully utilize the capacity of the factory.[23] For the entire period of its operation, the factory generated only losses, and from 1862 until 1880 ate up not less than 38% of the profits made in Russia. As early as 1864 Werner had advised Carl to discontinue production in Chmelewo altogether. He had met with resistance, however, since Carl was stubbornly trying to make the factory profitable. But as the results turned from bad to worse, Carl finally had to carry out the liquidation. Gorodok was shut down on May 1, 1881. All in all, Chmelewo/Gorodok had caused a loss of about 830,000 rubles, equivalent to approximately two million marks.

Siemens & Halske sought to further expand its business in Russia by demonstrating the possibilities of constructing an electric railway. The company built a functioning electric railway "to demonstrate to the Russian public the use of electricity for the operation of railways." For this accomplishment Siemens & Halske received the highest possible decoration at a Moscow industrial exhibition, the imperial double eagle, which the firm was now authorized to use in its letterhead. For Carl, more important must have been the public demonstration that Siemens & Halske was present in the Russian market again, as dynamic as before and determined to promote the development of electrical technology in Russia to the fullest extent.

New opportunities in telegraphy beckoned. In 1881 the Russian government planned to run two parallel cables from Odessa to Sebastopol, and from there one cable to Batum on the eastern coast and one to Varna on the western coast of the Black Sea. The total value of the order for cables amounted to a large sum, from £150,000 to £200,000, or as much as 4 million marks. In spite of the government's desire "to have the cables manufactured on credit," Siemens & Halske was very interested in obtaining the commission.[24] Carl Siemens, however, had reason to be fearful that the current and future contracts for cables would be won by their competitor, the Great Northern Company in England, because of personal interests of the official in charge of awarding the contracts. For Carl, the most effective way to eliminate competition was to construct a Siemens & Halske cable factory in St. Petersburg, a project that had been planned since 1878. Carl could count on cooperation from the Russian government, because the Russian Department of the Navy needed considerable quantities of rubber-insulated wires, which up to that time had been produced by the London branch of Siemens in the cable factory in

Woolwich. The Department of the Navy had wanted a domestic source, so as to be independent of imports in case of a war.

Carl's plan to have the company's third cable factory built in St. Petersburg met with some opposition at first, since the temporarily vacant cable factory in Berlin caused Werner some concern.[25] Carl overcame this reluctance by emphasizing the favorable prospects offered by having a cable factory in Russia and, at the same time, by estimating the necessary financial outlay to be quite small. Carl seriously underestimated the investment necessary, however, as shown in the balance sheets of the St. Petersburg factory for the next few years, which indicate large amounts of money charged for the cable factory. Later developments, however, corroborated his prediction about earnings. After just seven years, the profits made had already exceeded the initial investment. The problem of temporary underemployment in the cable factory was solved by entering the production of burners for the "regenerative" lamps for illumination based on gas, invented by Friedrich Siemens.[26]

The company also benefited from the introduction of the electric lamp in Russia. The final agreement on the production of incandescent lamps in Russia was reached during the negotiations for the founding of the AEG Corporation (Allgemeine Elektrizitäts-Gesellschaft) in Germany. This arrangement stipulated that AEG in Russia would buy all lamps produced by Siemens & Halske in St. Petersburg at preferential prices. In return Siemens & Halske had to pay 30 pfennigs per lamp to the Société Continentale (an Edison Company) in Paris.[27]

Apart from cables and accessories for electric lighting such as lighting fixtures, switches, and fuses, Siemens & Halske in St. Petersburg produced equipment for railway safety systems (safety interlocks for switches and track sectioning provisions, for which it even enjoyed a monopoly). In addition, there were orders for the telegraph business and for the construction of Morse and Hughes type telegraphs. When the Russian government raised import tariffs considerably, in 1883 Siemens also started local production of electric generators and motors. In that year 31 units totaling 91 horsepower were manufactured; in 1896, 544 units totaling 6,737 horsepower were produced.

Following the death of his brother Werner in 1892, Carl

started to participate in the management of the entire enterprise and moved his residence to Berlin in 1894. On June 1, 1898, the Petersburg division of the firm went public, a plan Carl had harbored for some time. The existing facilities were incorporated into the newly founded Russian Electrotechnical Corporation Siemens & Halske, St. Petersburg.

During this period the organizational structure of the Russian business was simple. Though often referred to as the "merchant" among the Siemens brothers, Carl in fact had a low opinion of strategic ideas in business management and called William Meyer, who showed a tendency to think along such lines, an "enormous philistine."[28] For this reason the organization of the efforts in Russia relied primarily on improvisation and on the personal initiative of the managers of the branch offices or agencies. This concept was so successful only because there could be no doubt whatsoever of Carl's loyalty to the parent company in Berlin. Similarly, the officials in major positions, responsible for the installation of the telegraph lines and for their maintenance, were closely connected with the Siemens family personally and thereby occupied a position of trust. This personal, improvised style of organization offered the great advantage of enabling the enterprise to adapt rapidly without major problems to the quickly changing conditions and highly fluctuating volume of the Russian business. But although initially acceptable, in the medium term this structure proved to be disadvantageous, because after expiration of the maintenance contracts and Carl's departure from St. Petersburg, Siemens & Halske did not have a satisfactory management upon which to fall back.

Start of the London Branch

In the years after the Nottebohm crisis the engagement in England became the second important pillar of the young Telegraph System Construction Enterprise. The initial conditions in England were fundamentally different from those in Russia. In 1850 England was by far the most industrialized country in the world and had a highly developed telegraph technology of its own. Accordingly, innovative and superior technology offered a means to carve out only a small business volume in niches of the market. Unlike in Russia, private companies operated the telegraph network in England, where no national telegraph authority existed. The private firms that installed and maintained the telegraph system resorted to the highly developed London capital market for their financing. As an example, in 1846 the Electric Telegraph Company was able to raise a sum of £140,000 for the patents held by William Cooke and Charles Wheatstone.[29] In 1838 the railway companies had already awarded the contracts for installation of the first inland line and were therefore highly interested in rapid completion. Unlike on the continent of Europe, the military use of the telegraph network, which was nationalized in 1870, played only a minor role.

Nonetheless, the companies operating the telegraph lines were in many respects subjected to strict state control. By issuing licenses the government controlled the installation of lines and prevented direct competition on individual lines. For government dispatches the British government reserved the right to special terms (half price, priority transmission of messages), and in case of war even the right to confiscate the telegraph lines in England and in the British protectorates. In exchange, the operating companies were subsidized by government funds. Because of the closed structure of the system, it was extremely difficult for small or foreign companies to gain access to the English market. The Electric and International Telegraph Company, which resulted from the merger of the Electric Telegraph Company and the International Telegraph Company, remained undisputedly dominant in the inland market.

In spite of this situation, Werner wanted to do business in Britain. He recognized the importance of English patents and of a name well known in England for sales on the world market. Thus he had tried to market his earliest inventions there. His brother Wilhelm had supported Werner in these efforts and had made an important contribution to the technology of cable insulation by passing samples of gutta-percha on to his brother.

Soon after 1848 and the founding of Siemens & Halske, Wilhelm and Friedrich had professionally and financially withdrawn from their business relationships with Werner in favor of their own developments in mechanical engineering and thermal technology. Thus the collaboration between Werner and Wilhelm took an entirely different form from the one between Werner and Carl, which proved so successful in Russia. Wilhelm was unwilling to subordinate his work and interests completely to the "family business" of his brother. This fundamental stance and the high prices of the products made in Berlin were certainly responsible for the nature of the relationship between the London and Berlin Siemens firms, which was not always unproblematic.

Nevertheless, there was a continuing relationship between Werner in Berlin and Wilhelm in England. In 1850 Wilhelm signed a contract with Siemens & Halske that made him an authorized business agent. However, rising expenses were initially not balanced by income, and accordingly this form of cooperation did not seem to be very promising. Wilhelm was unable to spend more than a small part of his working hours on his activities as an agent for Siemens & Halske. After Friedrich in particular had worked in London since 1848, and then again after the 1851 world exhibition, on Werner's improvements of the Wheatstone type pointer telegraph and for the entire manufacturing program of Siemens & Halske—although without substantial economic success—the brothers considered a new business strategy. For some time, direct investments in England were planned, for example, the construction of a factory for processing gutta-percha.

Within the scope of his scientific activities, Wilhelm had in the meantime turned his interest toward a specialized area: the production and laying of maritime cables for telegraphy. Access to the market in this sector proved to be difficult also, however. The idea of providing connections for telegraphy via submarine cables had been vigorously pursued in England since the 1840s, particularly since the discovery of the process for insulating cables with gutta-percha had solved one of the key problems. As early as 1845 the General Oceanic Telegraphic Company was founded in England with the intention of laying the first transatlantic cable between England and America.

The plans of the brothers John and Jacob Brett to connect England with the Continent via a submarine cable were of a less ambitious nature. They succeeded in obtaining a concession from the French government for the landing point of the cable. In 1850 they placed the first operational telegraph cable between Dover in England and Cape Gris-Nez in France, but the cable proved to be of poor durability and broke on the day after its inauguration. Next the Bretts ordered a special submarine cable to be produced by the wire rope factory R. S. Newall & Co. This cable not only contained insulated copper wires but in addition was sheathed with a reinforcing outer layer of steel wires. In 1851 this cable was laid between Dover and Calais and made the Brett brothers and the supplier of the cable, R. S. Newall, famous overnight. The Brett enterprise won numerous subsequent contracts for cables between England and Ireland, England and Belgium, and for supplying submarine cables to the French and Italian governments. Until the mid-1850s the Brett enterprise was the undisputed market leader in this field.

In the face of such formidable competition, Siemens & Halske's only feasible access to the submarine cable business was via indirect approaches. It was advantageous in this situation that Wilhelm Siemens had earlier established close contacts with Lewis Gordon, a partner in the firm R. S. Newall. Gordon was a professor of engineering at Glasgow University whom Wilhelm had met in engineers' clubs in London, which he frequently visited. Wilhelm struck up a friendship with Gordon, and eventually became his brother-in-law when he married Lewis's sister Anne in 1859.

The first business connection between Newall & Co. and the Siemens brothers was established in 1853, when Newall &

Co., shortly before the outbreak of the Crimean War, had supplied and delivered the submarine telegraph cable for the route St. Petersburg–Oranienbaum–Kronstadt in Russia. Since 1857, mediated by Professor Gordon, the opportunity opened up for cooperation beyond the initial agreement to buy each others' products. Newall & Co. had been awarded the contract to lay a submarine cable between Sardinia and Algeria, a project requiring an expert partner for testing the cables. As the Bretts had previously failed twice with this line, Newall & Co. decided to follow Gordon's recommendation and authorize Siemens & Halske to perform the acceptance tests on the cables and also to supply the necessary telegraphs. Werner von Siemens himself took part in the laying of the cables and, beyond his actual assignment to check the cables, developed an improved procedure for laying them, employing a brake mechanism based upon exact calculations, which was used while the cable was being paid out from the cable-laying ship. This innovation contributed to the successful completion of the contract.

A breakthrough had now been achieved into the English market, and subsequent orders for the cooperating partners Newall and Siemens soon followed. In contrast to the English methods of practical, pragmatic experimentation by trial and error, Werner von Siemens succeeded in winning a reputation as a technician proceeding along scientific principles, a status he cherished. Much later, he published with the Berlin Academy of Sciences (Berliner Akademie der Wissenschaften) the insights he had acquired in the process of laying cables.[30]

Following the first Sardinian line, Newall and Siemens in 1857 successfully carried out more cable laying in the Mediterranean. In doing so they had, for the time being, succeeded in displacing Brett completely from the business to establish an important market position for themselves. Just one year after the company's slowdown after completion of the Russian orders during the Crimean War, this new situation gave Werner von Siemens reason to be optimistic: "It is obvious that combined with Newall we form a force that cannot be pushed aside or bypassed easily. It would serve the interests of both Newall and ourselves to publicize this association. Each one has its circle of followers, and ours is not that small—most likely we would contribute Austria, Holland, and Russia, and all three countries have great plans, above all Holland in the East Indies."

Once Siemens had successfully penetrated the English market with its underwater technology, the brothers reorganized their firm. They converted the London branch into an independent entity in 1858 with the brothers Werner and Wilhelm Siemens, Georg Halske, and the firm Newall & Co. as partners. The new firm was named Siemens, Halske & Co. with the intention of expressing by the name the close ties to the parent firm in Berlin. Wilhelm was also supposed to run a separate firm for the production of materials for telegraphy in London to circumvent the high import duties on electrical and mechanical instruments. (When the Cobden Treaty, representing an agreement on greatly extended free trade between England and the states on the Continent, was later signed, these protective tariffs were abolished.) At the end of 1858, with support from Berlin, Wilhelm set up a small factory employing between eighty and a hundred workers at Millbank Row, Westminster, ready to go into immediate production. This facility remained in existence until 1866, when it was incorporated into a larger firm.

Entirely in accordance with Werner's plans, participation in the English cable business took a dynamic course; the planned permanent cooperation with Newall, however, came to a sudden end. In 1860 the contract initially intended to be valid for a period of five years was terminated owing to a never ending series of disagreements. Siemens had pledged to buy Newall cables exclusively. The high prices asked for these cables, however, made it impossible for Siemens to match the bids of other competitors. In 1858 and 1859 the two business partners still successfully carried out some orders, for example, laying cables from Constantinople to the islands of Chios and Crete, from Syros to Chios, and from Crete to Alexandria, and finally a partial stretch of the telegraph line to India through the Red Sea and the Indian Ocean.

Because of continuing tensions in the business relations

with Newall, Werner von Siemens began to look for a new English partner and considered the cable producer Glass & Elliot.
Wilhelm, however, strongly advised against such a liaison,
since he believed Glass & Elliot to enjoy neither a high reputation nor a sufficient financial base. In 1860 Siemens & Halske
nevertheless terminated the contract with Newall, paid a pen-
alty of £1,000, and even had to authorize Newall to continue
using the Siemens test procedures. But without its German
partner the cable company was not able to stay in the market
for long and soon discontinued its production of submarine
telegraph cables altogether.

Werner and Wilhelm Siemens, who had been appointed
personal advisers on deep-sea cables to the English government, found themselves in a position to continue business
without their English partner. Wilhelm, who had become a
naturalized citizen on March 19, 1859, the day of his engagement to Anne Gordon, and subsequently used the anglicized
form of his name (Charles William Siemens), was thus able to
make good use of his contacts in engineering circles and with
the authorities for the benefit of the company.[31] Through his
contacts with the British Department of Trade, he, together
with Werner, succeeded in winning a contract with the British
government entrusting Siemens & Halske by July 13, 1859,
with checking all governmental cables, as almost all British
submarine cables had proved to be incapable of functioning.
This government contract at last signified for Siemens full access to the English market. Wilhelm's having become a naturalized British citizen did not, however, cause the London
business of Siemens to be regarded as an English enterprise,
and the government's awarding of the contract to Siemens resulted in protests in the English trade journals.

After the separation from Newall & Co. the Siemens brothers were in need of a new cable supplier. Not wishing to tie
themselves exclusively to an English partner again, they considered establishing a cable factory of their own in England.
Wilhelm also encouraged his brother Werner to enter directly
into the operation of telegraph lines, that is, to engage in the
business of a contractor. The Malta-Alexandria line appeared

to be a suitable project in this area, since because of the high risks involved, the British government did not want to continue operating this line itself. After very promising negotiations the takeover did not materialize, however, as the cable manufacturer Glass & Elliot undercut Siemens & Halske. Even the sizable advance in trust that the German enterprise enjoyed in dealing with the British government, based on its successful activities in laying and checking cables, was unable to outweigh the considerably more favorable terms submitted by the domestic competitor. In the operation of the Malta-Alexandria line Glass & Elliot made a great deal of money and substantially improved its position in the market. Wilhelm Siemens was quite annoyed that his brother Werner and Georg Halske had spoiled this business opportunity by submitting an excessively conservative and cautious bid: "By losing the operation of the Malta-Alexandria line, we have yielded the dominant role in the market to Glass & Elliot and have reduced our business here to zero, or, to be more precise, to a loss of £200 per month."[32]

Wilhelm saw only one chance to stay in business in the future: a forced entry into the deep-sea cable business. Only in this section of the telegraph business was there as yet no saturation of the English market. Intercontinental telegraph lines, such as, for example, the connection from England to India or to America, required huge capital expenditures, since they were not financed by national authorities but by private operator companies. Accordingly, the risks run by such enterprises were high, particularly in the face of the comparatively new and still undeveloped technology for laying submarine cables. Admittedly, there were also other profitable opportunities for the London business, such as the construction of a transmission line in South Africa connecting Cape Town with Delagoa Bay, a commission worth £20,000.

An assessment of the overall business situation—for many years consisting only of maintenance work in Russia and sustained stagnation in Germany—quickly revealed that the prospects for major orders were not very favorable. Within the company two distinct factions rapidly formed: Wilhelm

Siemens regarded the laying of undersea cables both as an attractive technical challenge and as a profitable prospect in the market and was ready to take the risk. Although basically more risk averse, Werner was likewise fascinated by the technical task and, moreover, willing to support his brother. Halske in the end shied away from the large financial risk and also opposed any uncontrolled expansion of the business, which so far had been conducted within the limits of the conventional trades. Halske was nevertheless persuaded, even though hesitatingly, to agree to a first step: starting in 1863, the London branch opened a cable factory of its own in Charlton, near Woolwich, in order to become independent of the quality levels and price structures of external suppliers.

Thanks to his personal contacts with the director general of the French telegraph authority, Monsieur de Vougie, Werner had succeeded in acquiring a commission awarded by the French government which gave Siemens & Halske the first opportunity to lay a submarine cable between Cartagena (Spain) and Oran, using their own material. This project, however, turned out to be a complete failure: in the course of two attempts the cable was lost; moreover, the cable-laying ship was damaged. This was all the worse, as the brothers had risked their reputation on this order. Werner and Wilhelm had both traveled to the site in order to take personal charge of the laying of the cable. In addition to the financial losses, amounting to £150,000—half of the firm's capital—the brothers suffered a considerable loss of personal prestige.[33]

For Johann Georg Halske, this failure offered a welcome opportunity to terminate his participation in the English part of the business, which he had always disliked. He even demanded the complete dissolution of the English enterprise and received support in this matter from Werner's friend William Meyer, who held power of attorney in the company. In this situation, only Werner's vision of the bond linking the members of the family and his dream of a "worldwide business" saved the English branch. In the case of a complete retreat by the parent company in Berlin, Wilhelm Siemens would hardly have been in a position to continue by himself alone the

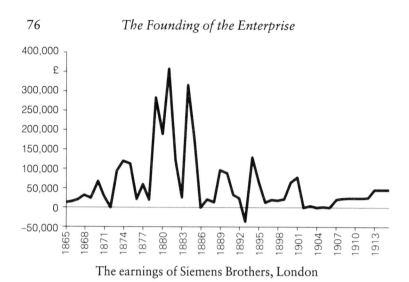

The earnings of Siemens Brothers, London

business in England, heavily burdened by considerable losses, all the more as his main interest was not in telegraphy. While Werner had to accept Halske's desire to resign from the English branch, he was not willing to let Wilhelm down. Meanwhile, the tense atmosphere that had developed between the offices in London and Berlin made the negotiations over the new organization of the enterprise difficult. Wilhelm was willing to cooperate with his brothers, but he bluntly rejected any ties with Berlin. Even before the fundamental disagreement with Halske, Werner's idea of a "comprehensive enterprise," the individual branches of which would subordinate themselves to the integrated whole organizational body whose center would be Berlin, met with Wilhelm's opposition.[34]

The restructuring of the London business, which was continued as of January 1, 1865, under the name Siemens Brothers, proved to be tedious and difficult. Wilhelm and Werner had fundamentally different views on the relationship between Berlin and London. Wilhelm's main concern was to have free scope in his business policy: the London enterprise should be at liberty either to produce its own devices and instruments or to order them from Siemens & Halske in Berlin, or indeed

The Siemens Brothers cable factory, Woolwich

A cable-assembling machine, Siemens Brothers, Woolwich

from any other firm. This was a demand that did not meet with Werner's approval at all:

> Your suggestion will ultimately result in the establishment of two competitive businesses, one here and one in London. Whereas I myself manage and own this one here alone, I am supposed to be a silent partner in the competing London business. I am convinced that upon second thought you too will come to the conclusion that this represents an impossible position for me. . . . I therefore ask you to consider in the future only the two alternatives—complete unification or total separation of our interests in telegraphy. I will never agree to a poorly defined intermediate position.[35]

As Werner had by far the stronger financial base, he was eventually able to demand a certain degree of linkage between the independent London firm and Siemens & Halske in Berlin. The difference of views held by Wilhelm and his closest associate in London, Ludwig Löffler, and Werner as the main supplier of capital on the relationship to Berlin repeatedly caused serious tensions in the "comprehensive enterprise." Additionally, as Halske remained adamant in his decision eventually to withdraw from the Berlin business in 1867, as planned, and as the Russian maintenance contracts were due to expire in the same year, the prospects for the three main pillars of the Siemens enterprise—in Berlin, St. Petersburg, and London— were extremely precarious in 1865–66.

Crisis and Restructuring

Thus the cable-laying fiasco and Halske's withdrawal from the London business created something of a crisis for the Siemens firm, the causes of which were much deeper than a single business setback. The senior executives of both enterprises abroad—and in this respect Carl for once agreed with Wilhelm—reproached the parent firm in Berlin. Wilhelm and Carl complained about fundamentally unprofessional management, inflexibility, and a jealously guarded claim to dominance. As an example, Berlin, because of its old-fashioned technology of manual production, was unable to avoid delays in filling large orders, such as the contract awarded for the Russian lines, for the business with Newall, or for sideline jobs such as the production of water meters for the English market. In spite of these management problems, senior business executives in Berlin, including Johann Georg Halske and even Werner von Siemens himself, became highly irritable any time the other brothers looked around for alternative suppliers, or even suggested setting up production facilities of their own. Werner always tried to be open-minded toward his brothers' views, yet he was so preoccupied with the idea of a "comprehensive Siemens enterprise" and an "integrated whole organization" that he was incapable of accepting any sensible business arguments that even remotely endangered his principal idea of a closely knit family enterprise under his guidance and operating worldwide. The conflict that arose between Werner's vision of a worldwide family firm and the needs of operating managers in foreign countries would provoke a great deal of tension in the years to come.

In the immediate crisis, Werner eventually forced his ideas upon his brothers. Wilhelm Siemens reacted by reconcentrating on his engineering activities. Together with his brother Friedrich he kept himself busy with the development and refinement of the Siemens-Martin process for the production of steel, a technology he introduced to the public in 1868 at a session of the Chemical Society in London. This open-hearth furnace was to revolutionize the technology of steel manufacturing around the world.[36] In the execution of the next major project won by Siemens Brothers, the Indo-European telegraph line, Wilhelm left the planning and construction largely to his brothers.

Carl's relationship to Werner was less complicated, even though his relationship to Berlin did not remain totally unspoiled. Carl had, with little success, invested the profits from the Russian maintenance contracts into various business ventures. In 1864, with Werner's consent, he had even bought a copper mine in Kedabeg in Georgia, near the Caucasus

Mountains. The lack of follow-up orders in St. Petersburg and his string of failures in other business attempts (except for the alcohol meters, mentioned above) made the liquidation of the St. Petersburg business more and more probable after the expiration of the maintenance contracts in 1867. Werner would have liked to see his brother again work as a senior executive in Berlin or London. However, in part in consideration for his wife, who suffered from a lung disease, Carl preferred to settle down in Tbilisi in the south of the Russian empire. There he devoted his time to the management of the copper mine in Kedabeg and to the negotiations for the construction of the Indo-European telegraph line.

Werner von Siemens experienced considerable distress at such "plans for disengagement from the business." Siemens & Halske had never succeeded in gaining a foothold abroad without the direct commitment of loyal members of the family. The foundation of a subsidiary in Vienna in 1858, to which Siemens had been urged by the Austrian government, had been an attempt in that direction. Because of the boom in the construction of railways, the prospects for making profits were good. In addition, the chance to establish a bridgehead in the Balkans, in Greece and Turkey, was tempting. For such a line, as part of the line to India, Werner intended to establish an operating company to finance the enterprise. The Berlin company official Steinert was appointed executive manager of the Vienna branch, but he proved inadequate to the task. In the first two years sales were low; then Steinert accepted more orders than could be filled by the Vienna facilities and thus lost many customers who became irritated by the poor quality of the products delivered and by late shipments. In 1864 the Vienna branch had to be liquidated with losses.[37]

In the face of the bitter experience in Austria, Werner was more interested than ever in seeing members of the family as senior executives wherever possible. He paid little attention to the fact that Wilhelm at least had in the meantime outgrown the overprotective "guidance" of his brother Werner. After developing the electromagnetic generator in 1866, then called the dynamomachine, and conducting preliminary negotiations for the major project of the Indo-European telegraph line, Werner spent most of his business efforts on reorganizing his enterprises. His attention was all the more necessary because of Johann Georg Halske's retirement from the firm on December 31, 1867.

In a set of agreements dated August 23 and August 24, 1867, Werner succeeded in promulgating three important signposts for the future conduct of the business as "the comprehensive Siemens enterprise":

1. Halske left a large part of his capital as a loan to the firm, which accordingly did not suffer a sudden decrease of capital.
2. Siemens & Halske, Berlin, as well as Siemens Brothers, London, were taken over at common cost and were to be run in the future as joint enterprises. The independent firm in St. Petersburg was liquidated and continued as a branch of the Berlin enterprise in the legal form of a limited partnership.
3. Following Halske's departure, the brothers Wilhelm and Carl were appointed as sole partners of the main enterprise and committed themselves to long-term work as chief executives: Wilhelm as director of the London firm, Carl with temporary residence in Tbilisi.

With the implementation of the "comprehensive Siemens enterprise" Werner had pushed through his basic ideas. As a concession to his brothers, the agreements gave each brother the right to conduct additional business on his own account. Wilhelm was allowed to continue his engineering firm, whereas Carl, together with Werner and a younger brother Walter, managed the mining business, with Carl continuing to reside in Tbilisi. Moreover, Werner was generous as far as the distribution of the profits was concerned. Wilhelm and Carl were allocated shares of the profit far surpassing the percentage of their contributions to the firm's capital: Werner was to receive 40%, Wilhelm 35%, and Carl 25% of the profits.[38] This arrangement, which apart from insignificant modifications—for example, in the size of the profit shares—remained in force until 1880. Tedious negotiations in the form of letters between London, Berlin, and St. Petersburg preceded the final agreement. Werner's efforts to persuade Carl to leave his somewhat remote residence in Tbilisi and to accept a position in Berlin or London were not successful until the death of Carl's wife, Marie. Werner only reluctantly tolerated the private business activities of his brother:

> The problem is that you then will be completely absorbed by our private business (Tbilisi). This is certainly very advantageous for me, but definitely not in the interest of our other partners. This is the bad side effect of private business activities of individual partners! I would have preferred to seize the opportunity to achieve a unification of the whole enterprise, of course with the allocation of the profits of the whole enterprise to the individual partners reflecting the actual conditions and circumstances.[39]

Twenty years after the founding of Siemens & Halske, Werner had succeeded, after all, in keeping together the telegraph business, which was by now operating on a worldwide scale, to be entirely owned and operated by the family. By arranging for joint accounting, the parent firm in Berlin maintained its leading position, although with the Indo-European telegraph line and additional cable business, the London firm showed an increasing importance. The entire enterprise, which in the meantime had achieved considerable sales, still had a comparatively unsophisticated organizational structure. Major projects were initiated and supervised solely by members of the family. The management of the daily business in London and Berlin was entrusted to a few long-term employees, such as Löffler in London and Haase in Berlin. As the only concession made to mass production, piecework was introduced in Berlin in 1858.[40]

Inevitably, however, there was change in the management and in the personnel of the firm in Berlin. Werner's close business associate and friend William Meyer, who had held power of attorney for Siemens & Halske since 1855, fell severely ill in

1867 and was employed only informally until his death in 1868. After the onset of Meyer's illness and Halske's withdrawal from the firm, Werner von Siemens was finally forced to start delegating assignments for design and development to engineers specifically hired for that purpose.

The lack of a formal organizational structure and the conduct of management almost exclusively by family members had had great advantages during the period of early growth. Only in retrospect, from the perspective of twentieth-century business practices, is Werner's desire to have the business controlled on the basis of kinship unusual. Conducting a business enterprise through family members was typical before the growth of huge enterprises and the resulting need to develop cadres of professional managers. For Siemens & Halske, loyalty and absolute personal commitment were of inestimable value in a line of business relying almost exclusively on only a few, mostly governmental, customers. Running the business without cumbersome organizational structures facilitated maximum flexibility and enabled the brothers to easily begin new activities after failures that had not resulted in large losses.

The expansion in the range of products following diversification into the use of electric power, and the steady increase in the volume of funds required for the telegraph and undersea cable business, required skilled business planning for the next twenty years, however. The firm needed to base its business planning on a more differentiated organizational structure. In this context, after 1867 Siemens & Halske began to borrow funds from banks. Earlier the services of banks had been utilized only for the transfer of profits from activities abroad and for the short-term bridging of temporary financial shortages. Siemens & Halske thus entered a new phase in its history.

4

The Enterprises of the Siemens Brothers to 1889

General Survey

Beginning in 1866 the business of Siemens & Halske expanded considerably as a result of new orders. The company's expansion began well before the business boom that followed the Franco-Prussian War and the unification of Germany in 1870. In the course of this enormous overall economic boom, which lasted to 1873, the workforce of the Berlin firm rose from 166 in 1866 to 628 in 1873.[1] At the same time, the buildings of the factory at the Markgrafenstraße site in Berlin were considerably enlarged. Werner von Siemens had a second factory built in Charlottenburg, then a suburb of Berlin, and transferred the production of nontelegraphy articles—for example, the assembly of alcohol meters—to that new facility.

Several major orders were the reason for this upswing. The Indo-European telegraph line and the laying of the transatlantic cable in cooperation with Siemens Brothers in London were important projects for Siemens & Halske, as were orders from the Prussian military authorities triggered by the Franco-Prussian War (1870–71). The relationship between Siemens and the Prussian state telegraph authorities had improved after Nottebohm retired in 1857, and Siemens had reestablished co-

84

The factory yard, Markgrafenstraße, Berlin, ca. 1870

operative relations with Nottebohm's successor, Colonel von Chauvin. Growth of Siemens & Halske accelerated substantially after 1875, moreover, when the new German Reich integrated the administration of the telegraph system into the comprehensive postal administration of the newly created empire, the German Reich. The office of the postmaster general, a position first held by Heinrich von Stephan—a great admirer and friend of Werner von Siemens—established a central, distinct authority for awarding major orders. Despite the tight

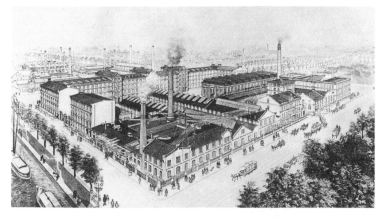

The Charlottenburg factory, ca. 1895

Activities of Siemens & Halske in Berlin, 1886

financial situation of the fiscal authorities of the empire during the so-called Founders Crisis (also called the Founder's Folly) after 1873, von Stephan promoted the construction of a network of telegraph lines based on underground cables. Accordingly, in 1876 Siemens & Halske founded its own cable factory in Berlin, which, unlike the English facilities in Woolwich, met the requirements of the authorities of the Reich for domestic production. Thanks to these orders, Siemens & Halske was able to record continually rising business in the 1880s, as domestic German business offset setbacks resulting from the expiration of international contracts.[2]

Less important for the momentary fortunes of the firm, but of great significance for its future, was Werner von Siemens's discovery in 1866 of the principle of the self-excited generator, a dynamo that permitted the efficient conversion of large amounts of mechanical energy into electric energy. Siemens's invention of the self-excited generator made possible a "second industrial revolution" characterized by the use of electrical energy in transportation, lighting, and especially factory production. Siemens's discovery replaced the inefficient steel magnets of the first generators with electromagnets, and allowed the harnessing of water or steam turbines to produce large amounts of electricity inexpensively. Paving the way for modern electric power technology, Werner obtained patents in Germany and England in 1867 and secured a major position for his firm in the age of electricity. By the end of the nineteenth century, cities and harbors would be illuminated with electricity, electric traction applied to streetcars, and electric motors used to drive machines inside factories.[3]

Siemens & Halske did not start the large-scale commercial exploitation of electrical power technology for over a decade, however. Full commercial development awaited other technical advancements, by Siemens and others. Until the end of the 1870s, Werner remained unconvinced that electric lights would replace the gas illumination already installed in city districts and individual homes. He concentrated on using electricity to

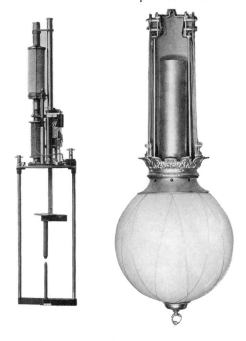

Arc lamp with carbon electrodes, ca. 1880

light large outdoor areas with arc lamps, rather than trying to employ lightbulbs using comparatively low wattage and fragile carbon filaments to produce relatively dim light.[4]

The economic recession in 1873 and the resulting slow-down in the growth of the overall economy did not adversely affect either the electrotechnical industry or Siemens & Halske. Siemens & Halske benefited from the general expansion of electric power technology; it also received additional orders for laying maritime and overland cables, particularly via the London branch of the enterprise, which boosted profits. Nevertheless, the company lost much of the clear edge it had once enjoyed over competitors. This setback was not due to a lack of technological progress but rather was rooted in the specific structure of the firm's top management, which was strongly dominated by a comparatively small circle of individuals. When those individuals, as we shall see, began to pay less direct attention to the company's affairs, Siemens & Halske suffered.

Between 1864 and 1867 Werner diverted his attention more to science and politics than to business. He also suffered a personal crisis after the death of his first wife, Mathilde, in 1865. In 1867, recovering from his loss, Werner von Siemens rededicated himself with all his energy to business management. Approximately at the time of Halske's withdrawal from business and the death of William Meyer, Werner hired some technical assistants in addition to the accountant Haase. Especially noteworthy was the employment of the engineer Friedrich von Hefner-Alteneck in 1867, inventor of the slotted rotor with distributed windings, still used over a century later, and of the differential arc lamp. Then in 1869 Werner von Siemens lured the telegraph engineer Carl Frischen away from the national telegraph service to work first on the Indo-European telegraph line and afterward for Siemens & Halske.[5] Finally, in 1873 the physicist Oscar Frölich was added to the staff. At first these key executives were allowed very little leeway, however. Werner harbored strong reservations about Frölich in particular, who sported a university education and an advanced degree.[6]

Werner's aversion to delegating authority and his strong mistrust of anybody not belonging to the family turned out to be an increasing hindrance to the company's international business. In Berlin alone, Siemens & Halske expanded from an at most moderately sized enterprise with 192 employees in 1867 to a large enterprise with 2,125 employees in 1889, the year Werner von Siemens retired from active business. Including the Siemens enterprises abroad, the workforce in 1889 totaled 4,513.[7]

Along with the expansion of the Berlin enterprise, business abroad increased also, but not at the same rate. The London enterprise was comparatively slow to engage in electric power engineering and relied more on the cable business. The relationship between Berlin and London continued to deteriorate, as Wilhelm declined to subordinate himself to the guidelines from Berlin. Wilhelm increasingly turned his attention to his scientific studies in engineering, leaving the management of Siemens Brothers more and more to his brother Carl, who in 1870 had moved to London in order to support Wilhelm, and to his authorized officer, Ludwig Löffler.[8] The tensions in the relationship with the parent firm in Berlin eased only when the London business was converted into a corporation after Carl had returned to Russia. Still, Werner regretted the reduction of his interests in London merely to financial affairs and the end of the close cooperation with the London enterprise.

The relationship between the Berlin and London firms was almost completely disbanded after Wilhelm's death in 1883. Serious disputes broke out with Ludwig Löffler, to whom Wilhelm had left a sizable parcel of shares of Siemens Brothers, a stake in the company that Löffler increased by buying more shares. Cooperation between the two firms became increasingly difficult, all the more as Löffler in the long run intended to split Siemens Brothers away from the rest of the enterprise. Arrangements on the subdivision of the world market, guaranteeing free scope to the London firm throughout the British Empire, remained in effect, however. Until World War I the Siemens enterprises in Berlin and London did not compete with each other on the world market.

Following Carl's return to Russia, business was reactivated there, although it never again assumed the decisive role it had enjoyed during the Crimean War. Carl was very open to the new electric power technology, and in St. Petersburg he sold huge illuminating installations (e.g., for lighting the magnificent Nevsky Prospekt and the Winter Palace), earning the company considerable prestige. Yet the renewed success in Russia did not last for long. After Werner's withdrawal from business, Carl unsuccessfully tried to liquidate the St. Petersburg business, and he returned to the Berlin board of management after Werner's death to support his nephews.

In addition to the branches in London and St. Petersburg, the Vienna branch also was finally successful, but another attempt to enter the market in Paris, this time in the field of lighting technology, failed. In 1878 the brothers rented rooms to establish a workshop of their own and founded from London the affiliated company Siemens Frères, but in 1886 they had to liquidate the firm with heavy losses. Relying on his personal reputation in France, Werner von Siemens had underestimated the intensity of anti-German sentiment on the French market after the Franco-Prussian War.

In the further expansion of business abroad, additional subsidiaries were no longer founded. Unlike the situation during the first stage of Siemens & Halske's activities, starting in the 1860s the volume of prefinanced government contracts decreased remarkably. In consequence, doing business as a contractor and developing a network of representative offices now turned out to be the two most important pillars of business abroad. Both forms of business were linked with some difficulties, however, as we shall see.

The Contracting Business

Doing business as a contractor became the most important arena in telegraphy after the 1860s. When Siemens & Halske functioned as a contractor, it either financed large facilities itself or set up a separate enterprise that would operate the telegraph system once it was built but that remained controlled by strategic decisions made in Berlin. The Indo-European telegraph line was the first big project handled by Siemens in this way.

The Indo-European Telegraph Line

The first telegraph line to India had been completed in 1860 by the Red Sea and India Telegraphy Company. During the period of cooperation between Siemens and Newall & Co., Werner von Siemens had personally participated in the installation of some sections as a testing engineer. The line suffered from numerous deficiencies, however. This was also true of two other lines routed overland, one via Persia and Russia, the other via Persia and Turkey, which had been in operation since 1865. As the telegrams had to be keyed in again at some of the intermediate stations, where the Persian or Russian operators frequently could not understand the content of the messages, the telegrams often arrived at their final destination in a garbled form incomprehensible to the recipient. Besides, as a result of the repeated rekeying of the telegrams, the speed of transmission was very low for both lines.[9]

Werner von Siemens thought of solving these problems by laying a new line transmitting the telegrams per induced current in a fully automatic way. Such a plan had been cherished by the brothers ever since 1865, but the implementation turned out to be difficult. Before they could deal with the technical problems, political problems had to be solved first. The British government, for example, was afraid of increasing the power of the czarist empire by running a line through Russia. The British also opposed the formation of any supranational telegraph network using individual national systems as components. Then the Prussian-Austrian War in 1866 interrupted the negotiations of the Siemens brothers for concessions. After the end of the war their position was permanently improved, however, since two men with whom Werner von Siemens had maintained close contacts had won executive positions in the telegraph business. In Russia, General von Lüders, who had acted as an intermediary for Siemens & Halske in the first business deal with Russia, became the new director general of the telegraph system in October 1866, and the Prussian official Colonel von Chauvin was appointed in the same year as director of telegraphy for the North German Confederation. Following a meeting between the directors of telegraphy— Champain (of the English-Indian Telegraph Administration), Chauvin, and Lüders, in April 1867—the Siemens brothers won the Prussian and Russian licenses for the laying of line. It was not yet possible for Siemens to lay a special cable from the Continent to England as part of the line, however, as Prussia had signed a contract with the Electric Company in England, granting the company the exclusive right to lay cables across that distance for several years. A similar agreement existed with the Reuter telegraph office for the former Hanoverian territory. Siemens finally succeeded in coming to terms with these two enterprises.

The negotiations with Persia, whose government made great efforts to avoid too great a dependence on Britain or Russia, proved to be particularly difficult. Moreover, the shah considered the telegraphy license a welcome source of income and tried to sell it at the highest possible price. As their negotiator, the brothers sent their second youngest brother, Walter, to Tehran. After the acquisition of the copper mine in Kedabeg, Walter Siemens had been employed in this "private business" by Werner and Carl, and had become familiar with eastern trading practices in Tbilisi. He was even appointed German consul in Tbilisi, and his brothers had allocated him 20% of the business in Kedabeg.[10] He carried out his commission in Tehran with great tenacity and skill. After negotiations lasting several months, Siemens won a license for the construction and maintenance of a telegraph line from Dzhulfa to Tehran at the turn of the year 1867/68.

After these first obstacles had been removed, the financing of the route had to be arranged. The Indo-European telegraph line was expected to become an economic success, but the technical details were still at an experimental stage, and running the line across four different sovereign territories involved numerous uncertainties. Werner's original plan to procure the necessary capital through private channels proved to be impossible to implement. Negotiations with the banker Amschel Mayer Rothschild, who was supposed to contribute three-quarters of the sum required, and parallel talks with the bankers Abraham Schaaffhausen and Gustav Mevissen did not succeed.[11] The Siemens brothers finally decided to finance the project via the stock market. To raise the capital, on April 8, 1868, the Indo-European Telegraph Company (IET) was founded as a public company based on English laws with a capital of £450,000. The Siemens brothers and Siemens & Halske together bought 20% of the shares; the remaining 80% were offered for sale in two equal parts in England and on the Continent. In addition, the Siemens brothers contributed their licenses and were in turn awarded the contract for the construction of the line for the lump sum of £400,000. For maintenance of the route Siemens was to receive £34,000 per annum. The sale of the shares proceeded swiftly in Germany but went slowly in England.

The Indo-European line was to be built by all branches of the Siemens organization. The facilities in Berlin and St. Petersburg would construct the line, while Siemens Brothers in London was to lay the maritime cables in the Black Sea and to supply the necessary materials. As the construction was to start on three sections simultaneously, aside from technical problems such as avoiding rekeying of telegrams, logistic problems in particular had to be solved. The paramount threat to the largest project Siemens had ever dared to undertake turned out to be a financial one, however. In summer of 1868 the World Telegraph Committee, founded in Paris three years earlier, met for a conference in Vienna to draw up technical regulations and the structuring of the fees. After Werner von Siemens's departure from the conference, the fee for telegrams from England to India was reduced from 87.5 to 71 French francs by the votes of his competitors, but also without any objection from the Russian director general of the telegraph systems, von Lüders. Additionally, the Persian government was supposed to collect a fee of 5 French francs for the stage from Dzhulfa to Tehran, and for the stretch between Tehran and Büshehr the British-Indian telegraph authorities were to receive a fee of 8.5 French francs.[12] These decisions knocked the bottom out of all the Siemens brothers' calculations about the profitability of the line, since in the face of such high expenditures for the licenses the construction of the line would be a money-losing operation. Even the offer from the Russian telegraph authorities to reduce their license fees could not reverse the situation.

Werner saw only one way out of this dilemma: to start negotiations in Persia again to have the additional fees canceled, or at least reduced. Under these circumstances, the death of Walter Siemens from an accident in the early summer of 1868 was a doubly heavy loss. A new negotiator for Persia, one enjoying the full confidence of the senior partner of the enter-

The Indo-European telegraph line, 1867–1870

prise, had to be sought. He was found in Georg Siemens—the son of Werner's cousin and previous partner—who at that time was active as the brothers' legal counsel. Georg Siemens proved to be a tough fighter: he stayed in Persia for eight months and ultimately threatened to sell the entire line to Great Britain. This threat finally achieved the desired result.

The company successfully completed the line's construction at the end of 1870. The site supervisors along the different sections of the line were competent, and Werner von Siemens allowed them more or less free scope to complete their tasks. The newly hired telegraph engineer Carl Frischen and Carl Siemens were responsible and prudent in their overall coordination of the construction.

The line was not opened immediately because of the extremely cold winter and the inadequate training of the staff in the use of the new system. The new system involved inputing telegrams via previously punched paper tapes, combined with the use of magneto inductors. This system eliminated the need for manual keying. Meanwhile, however, the British cable-laying ship *Great Eastern* had repaired the original maritime cable connection to India, and the price of IET shares had dropped to an extent demanding prompt action. On April 12, 1870, Wilhelm Siemens was able to offer a sensational demonstration in London: in the presence of prominent invited guests, an

Cable laying

exchange of telegrams between London and Calcutta covering a distance of 12,000 kilometers was completed within a single hour.

Accordingly, Werner von Siemens had achieved his technical aim: "to establish a long distance standard line and to get it working to show the true capabilities of present telegraphy."[13] Moreover, he had instantly become famous. Profitable operation of the Indo-European telegraph line was still by no means assured, however. On July 1, 1870, the maritime cable through the Black Sea was destroyed by an earthquake and had to be replaced by a new line on the mainland. But after re-opening in 1871, the line remained in operation until 1931, except for the World War I years. From the construction of the line, including repair and maintenance, the Siemens brothers received approximately the amount of profit they had expected. Payments of dividends based on their considerable monetary investment in the Indo-European Telegraph Company were initially few and far between, however. During the first years of business, the earnings barely covered the costs.[14] For this reason, the Siemens firms renounced for the time being the payout due to them and consented to the suspension of the dividends from their shares until the other stockholders had been paid a dividend of at least 10% of the price of their shares. In 1886 the dividend reached a level of 10%. In the long run the investment in the operating corporation turned out to be profitable; after the 1880s the telegraph company continually showed excellent earnings.

The Eastern Telegraph Company, operating the competitive line through the Mediterranean Sea, repeatedly tried to acquire IET. Finally, in 1877, despite initial resistance from

Paper-tape punching machine for the
Indo-European line

Prussia and Russia, a "joint purse arrangement" was set up, guaranteeing a preferred status for the Eastern Company and their undersea cables, while simultaneously assuring sufficient business for the Indo-European line. But as the undersea cables proved to be much more prone to defects, IET was several times in a position to transmit telegrams between Europe and India for months without any competition. This situation contributed considerably to IET's increased profitability.

Whatever the problems in financing and building the Indo-European line, Werner was committed to it for competitive reasons. As he explained to his brother Carl in the spring of 1870, before the project was finished: "Even if the shares should drop to half the price I paid for them, I nevertheless will invest all my disposable money in this project, since our fundamental strength is based on the exclusive concession for Russia and Prussia. The submarine lines will certainly get a punch."[15] As events turned out, not only was the venture profitable over the years, but it also added enormously to the reputation of the Siemens enterprises. In every respect, Werner's perseverance and self-confidence had paid off.

The Transatlantic Cable

Even more daring as a business venture than the construction and operation of the Indo-European telegraph system was the principal business activity of the London branch of the Siemens enterprises during the 1870s: the laying of submarine cables. Establishing a telegraph link between America and Europe was of supreme economic and political importance for the entire Western world. A successful solution of the problem promised enormous prestige. As a preliminary step, in 1855 a British government official, Frederick Newton Gisborne, had connected the extreme northeast of the American continent, Newfoundland, to the American telegraph lines on the mainland. Just one year later, an attempt was made to establish communication to Europe from Newfoundland. Venture capitalists were excited about the prospects. In 1856 a group of investors founded the Atlantic Telegraph Company with a capital base of £350,000. Cyrus Field, an American, bought £88,000 worth of the company's stock, and J. W. Brett, £12,000 worth; John Pender, later known as the "cable king," bought another parcel of stock for an undisclosed sum. The rapid sale of the stock indicated the urgency to establish such a line and the great willingness on both sides of the Atlantic to invest venture capital in it.

However, at that time the technology of laying cables was not at all perfected. Particularly in the field of deep-sea cables, development of the techniques to be used and of the design of the cables was still at an early stage, as the successful completion of such projects as well as the failures experienced by Newall & Co. and Siemens & Halske in the Mediterranean Sea proved. Likewise, the first attempts with a transatlantic cable had no lasting success, since the cable ruptured and sank. Nevertheless, the political interest in accomplishing the connection remained very strong, and the English Department of Trade and Commerce formed a commission that, with the help of a team of engineers from the Atlantic Telegraph Company, was to serve as troubleshooters. Wilhelm Siemens was one of the experts consulted in the matter.

Finally, in 1866 two cables were successfully connected to America. The project was financed by the successor of the Atlantic Telegraph Company, the Anglo-American Telegraph Company, in which Cyrus Field again had a decisive investment. In order to meet the demands of cable production, the cable manufacturer Glass & Elliot had consolidated with the Guttapercha Company to form the Telegraph Construction and Maintenance Company, with John Pender as chairman of the board. This company had subscribed to £315,000 of the estimated total cost of £600,000 for the production of the cables. Field chipped in the remaining £285,000. The two successful cable-laying operations had been preceded by a failed attempt, but efforts to salvage the cable that had sunk in 1865 were successful. At the beginning of the 1870s an additional cable was in operation, which extended from Brest in France via Newfoundland to Massachusetts, connected there in 1869 by the French Société du Cable Transatlantique Français.

Successful in this transatlantic venture, the Pender group sought to expand and began to move into a dominant position in the market. Pender tried several times to buy the Indo-European telegraph line. He bought facilities for the production of cables and expanded his influence over operating companies in order to secure for his trust, which he named Globe, a monopoly position wherever possible.

Carl Siemens proposed to his brothers to break the Pender monopoly by installing a transatlantic cable of their own. Carl was ending a period of mourning following the death of his wife, Marie, on February 1, 1869, and resolved to join in his brothers' London-based activities with full energy. The result was Siemens's decision to found a separate company to construct and operate a new transatlantic telegraph line. The contract for the venture would of course go to the Siemens brothers, just as it had with the Indo-European line. Unlike the existing cables routed via Newfoundland, Carl's plans called for a direct cable between Europe and America. For this reason, the company was to be called, in English, the Direct United States Telegraph Company (DUS). Because of the admittedly mixed experiences the Siemens enterprise had encountered in the laying of deep-sea cables, Werner von Siemens at first shied away from Carl's proposal for a new transatlantic venture. Wilhelm was also initially hesitant, as he had lost considerable amounts of money in conjunction with the attempt to lay a cable at North Africa between Cartagena and Oran. However, since Carl offered to dedicate all his energy to this project and also to supervise the laying of the cables himself, the brothers finally agreed. Again they founded a public company based on English laws. The shares of IET had sold slowly in England in 1868, and this time, owing to the enormous economic leverage of Pender's Globe, the prospects for attracting English capital were even smaller. The operating company was intended to be based on a capital of £1.3 million. The Siemens brothers themselves subscribed to a considerable number of shares. The Deutsche Bank in Germany, founded in 1870, went to great lengths to place the remaining stock. Georg Siemens, the successful negotiator in Persia, was now a director of the Deutsche Bank, an advantageous situation for the Siemens company. Georg Siemens strongly endorsed the project and even pledged to be liable with his own personal fortune for any transgression of the limit in funds he was authorized to commit. His pledge allowed the project to be funded and to go forward.

The work on laying Siemens's first deep-sea cables across the Atlantic started in 1873. The company planned to extend the cable from Ballinskelligs Bay in Ireland to Torbay in Nova Scotia. From there it would lay another leg to Rye Beach in New Hampshire, there connecting to the American lines on the mainland. The Woolwich factory, which under Carl's management had been expanded into a complete cable-producing plant, would manufacture the submarine cables. (Before 1871, work there had been limited to the stranding and armoring of cables, the final steps of cable production.)

Wilhelm designed a special ship for the most difficult part of the project, the actual laying of the cable. The cable-laying steamship *Faraday,* named on February 17, 1874, by Wilhelm's wife, Anne Siemens, soon entered service. The ship had 5,000 gross rated tonnage, was 360 feet long, and had a draft of 36 feet. The rear hold of the ship was large enough to accept 1,700 miles of cable.

The laying of the cables turned out to be an adventure. Many years later, Werner vividly recollected the various episodes and described them in several pages of his memoirs, written in 1891–92. Wilhelm Siemens and his manager personally participated in the project, as did Carl Siemens, who, as the head of the entire project, bore the brunt of the responsibility. Even Werner von Siemens traveled from Berlin to Ireland and Ballinskelligs Bay in order to supervise the first stages of cable laying.[16] There were many incidents during the laying of the cables. The first effort to lay the cable had to be aborted. Acts of sabotage and hoaxes, presumably staged by their competitor Globe, turned the operation into a nerve-racking affair. Carl claimed: "I can count the five years [in London] as ten lost years of my life. I have become a mental and physical wreck here."[17]

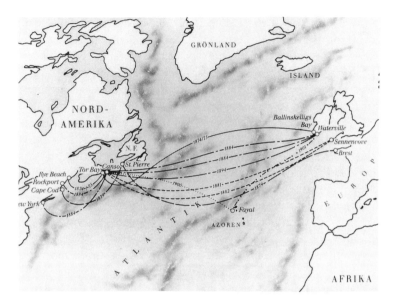

Cables laid in the North Atlantic by the *Faraday*

The cable-laying ship *Faraday*

Loading telegraph cable into the hold of the ship *Agamemnon*

As in the case of the Indo-European telegraph line, the brothers were ultimately able to deliver a technically perfect job: the Siemens transatlantic cable operated reliably and with a high rate of transmission. The business also proved profitable for Siemens Brothers in London. Despite numerous calls for improvements in the cable, the earnings of the London branch were reasonable, and a number of follow-up contracts in the wake of the success continued to assure a good outcome.[18]

The results for the operating firm were another story. The Direct United States Telegraph Company enjoyed no lasting success. Even a reorganization of the company, converting it into the Direct United States Cable Company, was unable to save the firm. The competition from the Pender trust turned out to be too strong and powerful. The operating firm ultimately had to concede and sell out to Pender. Georg Siemens suffered serious financial losses, as he had assumed personal responsibility for a considerable part of the stock issued by the company. Consequently, for some time the Globe group held a monopoly in the telegraph traffic between Europe and America, since in 1876 the French cable became inoperative.

Business as a contractor had therefore proved to be extremely risky for the telegraphy branch of the Siemens enterprise. With respect to the Indo-European telegraph line, the capital invested paid in the long run; as far as the DUS cable was concerned, losses had to be accepted. Werner von Siemens was well aware of the elements of instability in such projects. Contrary to his former partner Halske, however, he was willing to take such risks, not least in order to demonstrate the high level of technical proficiency of his enterprise. The projects involving submarine cables in particular remained risky for the time being. French and American companies formed as competitors to the Pender group and, following the successful laying of the DUS cable, awarded contracts to Siemens Brothers. These orders met with mixed results. The Siemens enterprise had serious difficulties in laying a cable off the Brazilian coast in 1874 and during the laying of a French Atlantic cable in 1879, a project personally supervised by Ludwig Löffler.

Cable laying was an arduous business. His experience with it moved Carl Siemens to observe that anybody active in the cable business would have to deal a lot with "hustlers and similar rascals."[19] The problems meant that the brothers were becoming sick of cables. With the conversion of Siemens Brothers into a public company in 1880 and the transfer of Carl Siemens back to Russia, the intensive involvement of the brothers in the cable business came to an end.

Cable laying continued under the direction of Ludwig Löffler, however, who took over the management of the London branch in 1883 after Wilhelm's death. Löffler successfully completed several further cable-laying contracts. In 1881 the firm was awarded a contract by the American "railway king" Jay Gould and in 1884 another contract by the Americans MacKay and Bennett, both for the laying of transatlantic cables. The transformation of the London branch into a public company owned mainly by the family but in which Löffler occupied a dominant position aggravated the existing conflict between London and Berlin. As discussed above, the roots of this conflict, which had appeared during Wilhelm's management of the London firm, lay in Werner von Siemens's perception of himself as the supreme head of the enterprise. This conflict, which was settled toward the end of the 1880s, will be dealt with in more detail in the next chapter.

Marketing Strategies in the Field of Electric Power

In the meantime, Werner von Siemens's main interest had shifted to the commercial use of electric power technology, where the business problems were very different from those encountered in telegraphy. His dynamomachine gradually became more efficient and dependable thanks to the inventions of Théophile Gramme and those of his own chief designer, Friedrich von Hefner-Alteneck. Illumination for military purposes and for the protection of coastal shipping (by lighthouses) were the only applications for this technology during the early years.[20] Around 1878 the technology had developed to a point where Siemens and other businessmen saw the feasibility of electricity's use in private and civilian markets. Lighting technology, electric railways, and electric motors useful in many fields began to offer wide areas for the application of electric power. In contrast to the telegraph business, a great number of small enterprises quickly entered the field of electric power technology, competing with Siemens & Halske in their individual specialties. Siemens and later AEG were the only "universal enterprises" in Germany active in all types of electrical technology. Another difficulty arose from the fact that different forms of application were competing with each other. Would electricity be delivered to customers as direct current or as alternating current? Indecision about the final choice of power delivery persisted for quite some time.

The absence of an agreed-upon technical standard was most evident in the field of lighting technology. First electric light had to face competition from gas light, and then the electric arc and the incandescent light competed with each other.

Initially, Werner von Siemens had placed all his confidence in the arc light, for which Siemens & Halske had carried out development work of its own. With his differential lamp Hefner had once more improved the arc light, which had become marketable on the base of advancements made by Pavel Yablochkov, a Russian living in Paris. Even before this further development of the technology, Siemens & Halske had in 1878 taken up negotiations with the Société Générale d'Electricité, founded by Yablochkov, in order to obtain the concession to erect arc light plants based on the Yablochkov principle. Siemens would have liked to enter the French market again by establishing a branch there, in order to get the full benefit of French patent protection. After Hefner's invention, Werner von Siemens was starting to doubt whether a contract with the Société would still make sense; yet in the middle of 1878 he signed a contract securing the French company half of the profits resulting from the installation of such plants and tying Siemens & Halske to their terms with respect to the price structure.

Mobile electrical lighting system, 1873

The success of Hefner's differential lamps meant that Werner was inclined to distance himself from the Yablochkov company, even though Yablochkov declared its willingness to employ generators made by Siemens & Halske instead of those made by its competitors. Werner was very keen to go into business dealing both with lamp production and with the production of generators for illuminating plants. The first experimental installation of arc lamps in Berlin in 1879 was successful, and Siemens secured follow-up contracts for the enterprise. Throughout, no central power plants were constructed, but individual generators were delivered and installed for each project. Consequently, financing via operating companies proved unnecessary for the time being.

Competition in the Electric Power Business

Preceded by a great publicity campaign, the incandescent light developed by Edison was demonstrated to the public in Paris in 1881. This presentation marked the end of the arc light era. Even Werner von Siemens ultimately could not shut his eyes to this development, although at first he had commented very critically on the incandescent light.[21]

Thomas Alva Edison marketed his inventions mainly by issuing licenses. His New York–based agency for issuing licenses in Europe was the Edison Electric Light of Europe Company, which in turn had four European subsidiaries. These branch companies were the Edison Light Company in London, holding the patent rights for England, and the Compagnie Continentale Edison in Paris, holding the rights for the rest of Europe. The task of the third company, the Société Electrique Edison, was the construction of central power plants; while the fourth company, the Société Industrielle et Commerciale, was in charge of the production of Edison's lightbulbs, machines, and other equipment. The latter companies were also located in Paris.

In order to take advantage of Edison's technology, Werner von Siemens became involved with Emil Rathenau (1838–1915), a businessman with great ambitions in the German electrical industry. Rathenau saw the incandescent light at the First International Electrical Exhibition in Paris in 1881. Deeply impressed, he promoted the idea of establishing a new German company to bring the Edison light to the German and European market. In 1882, with the help of many banks, Rathenau organized a commission to conduct experiments with Edison's illumination technology and to study its commercial introduction. Rathenau and his supporters soon realized that it would be desirable to convert the commission into a business holding the Edison licenses for Germany and operating systems for generating and distributing electricity to individual consumers. Rathenau did not think of this new enterprise as a competitor of Siemens & Halske, and he invited Werner von Siemens to participate in founding the new firm. The result was the creation of the German Edison Company for Applied Electricity (Deutsche Edison-Gesellschaft für Angewandte Elektrizität) (DEG), founded in March 1883. Siemens thought of DEG as a buyer of Siemens & Halske products and as a firm working for Siemens as an "installation agency."[22]

These expectations turned out to be a complete miscalculation, however. Siemens and Rathenau were pursuing fundamentally different business strategies, and the two men proved incompatible in bringing Edison illumination to the German market. Siemens & Halske was oriented more toward technical perfection than to earning the highest profits. Werner von Siemens, as we have seen, was cautious about expanding the business, and he always sought to do so in a way that maintained the control by family members. Emil Rathenau, in contrast, was an aggressive promoter who envisioned expanding into every aspect of electrical technology, and he was unwilling to accept a role as merely a buyer of Siemens & Halske products. Very quickly Rathenau sought to shake off the image of DEG as an installation agency for Siemens & Halske. He proceeded to take over the operation of the Berlin Electric Power Plants (Berliner Electricitätswerke), which soon served as a base for further expansion in the industry. He sought to enter or enlarge the presence of DEG in almost every field of electrical technology.[23]

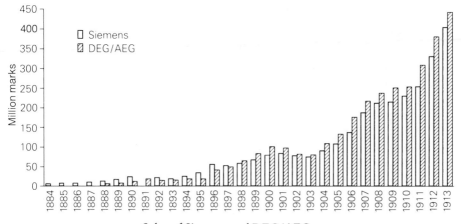

Sales of Siemens and DEG/AEG

The consequence of these maneuvers was the appearance in the German market of a major rival to Siemens & Halske, Rathenau's General Electric Company (Allgemeine Electricitäts-Gesellschaft) (AEG), as DEG was called after 1887. AEG at first engaged primarily in marketing licenses for the Edison patents for incandescent lamps.[24]

In addition to AEG, there was the firm Schuckert & Co., founded by Sigmund Schuckert (1846–95) in 1873, which developed from a small specialty enterprise for the production of floodlights to a concern with worldwide importance in power technology. In 1883 Schuckert recorded production of 233 generators and more than 1,000 arc lamps. In 1887 Schuckert began the erection of the first central electric power stations. Sigmund Schuckert proved to be a serious competitor. He had begun his career in the United States working with Edison, but he lacked that inventor's astuteness. Schuckert did not have the broad vision or the capacity for abstract thinking that Werner von Siemens enjoyed, nor did he have the entrepreneurial courage of Emil Rathenau. What distinguished Schuckert was a great knowledge of technology and a realistic view of the possibilities of marketing electricity and electrical products.[25] The result was that in the 1880s Schuckert & Co. was the most important large enterprise in the field of electric power engineering besides Siemens & Halske. In 1888 the Schuckert enterprise was reorganized into a limited partnership (*Kommanditgesellschaft*) and in 1893 into the public corporation Electricitäts-AG (EAG). In the 1890s the firm built and commissioned more central electric power plants (a total of 120 stations) than Siemens & Halske and AEG put together.[26]

Werner von Siemens was not altogether successful in responding to the appearance of these competitors. He reacted to the altered market situation by establishing capital companies intended to assure the future sale of Siemens & Halske products. He was unable, however, to win over German banks or financiers for a company named German Electrical Power Stations (Deutsche Elektrizitätswerke), designed to construct central electrical power plants abroad. Siemens & Halske offered to contribute one million marks to the capitalization of such a company, but this was not sufficient to entice further financing. Rathenau's strategy of buying a share in lighting companies seemed more promising to financiers. With the success of AEG, Siemens & Halske lost more and more ground in the lighting business in the second half of the 1880s.

The development of the telephone at about the same time also brought to the fore a potentially huge competitor to Siemens's telegraph business. The German postal service controlled telephone franchises in a way similar to its control of telegraphy. The postal service sought to foster competition in telecommunications, wanting a broad base of suppliers and favorable terms for equipment procurement. This policy meant that other rivals to Siemens & Halske appeared, including, in 1879, the firm Mix & Genest, and a few years later the forerunner of the German Telephone Works and Cable Industry (Deutsche Telephonwerke und Kabelindustrie AG).[27]

The Electrical Railway and the Construction of Power Plants

The successful electrification of the railways proved to be a difficult business problem. In 1867, shortly after the discovery of the electric dynamo, Werner had spoken out in support of electric streetcars as a worthwhile field for electrical locomotion. Electric traction in mines also seemed promising to him, because electric motors required no air supply and had no exhaust. At the Berlin industrial exhibition in 1879, Siemens & Halske presented the first electric locomotive, pulling several cars equipped with seats. While the locomotive met with great public interest, the sale of electric railways was another matter. For one thing, the technology demonstrated in 1879 was impractical. The locomotive received its power from a third central rail, grounded through the wheels on the other two rails. The exposed rails were hazardous: people and horses ran the risk of electric shocks. Municipal authorities imposed safety regulations to prevent shocks, and many projects did not materialize because of the technological limitations. The overhead pantograph power pickup was later developed in the middle of the 1880s by Frank Sprague in the United States, and it turned into a resounding success for him and for electric traction.

The financing of such projects was another problem. While Siemens & Halske was willing to participate in operating companies for electric railways, as it had done in the telegraph business, finding partners to finance electric street railways proved difficult. Efforts of Werner von Siemens to win the support of the Deutsche Bank for the founding of a German-Austrian railway company, intended to serve as a financing agency for Siemens & Halske, failed. Siemens offered to participate in this company and to sign over the revenue from the railway patents for Germany, Austria, Italy, and possibly also Russia, but to no avail.

By the 1880s the basic laws and principles for the use of electrical power technology had been discovered and developed, and the electrical industry considered the situation advanced enough to make electrical energy available throughout entire cities by means of block and central power plants. The companies active in this field, however, soon discovered that new forms of business were necessary to implement their far-reaching plans. The electrical industry faced a special problem:

Horse-drawn bus, Berlin, ca. 1850

Berlin streetcar, Spandauer Berg line, 1882

it had to create a demand for products that used the new technology. Usually, equipment suppliers, seeing the possibilities offered by inventions, developed products using advanced technology. It was then their task to make customers aware of their potential need for these new products. For almost all basic innovations a market had to be developed. This proved to be particularly difficult in this case, as electricity by itself is not a consumable commodity. Because of the novelty of electricity and their lack of experience in gauging its economic impact, municipal authorities held back on the allocation of contracts and agreed only to grant permission for the construction of electric power plants. Since the construction of power plants constituted a long-term tie-up of considerable amounts of capital, the involvement of financing and operating companies seemed the appropriate solution to financing problems. Such a company would operate separately, yet be under the influence of the parent firm.[28]

The trend in the German electrical industry, after ambitious men like Rathenau saw the possibilities of introducing Edison illumination, was for a firm to work simultaneously on several fronts. An electrical enterprise would function as the manufacturer of electrical equipment, as the supplier of electrical energy, and as a financing company. AEG pioneered this strategy, which other firms copied and took even further. This so-called contractor business, placing enormous demands on capitalization, promised huge profits from the expected future increase in the consumption of electrical energy.[29] Stimulated by the opportunities offered by the contractor business, the number of electric power plants in Germany increased between 1895 and 1900 from 180 to 774. Over the same period the number of electric railways rose from 47 to 156.[30]

In the long run, the conduct of the electrical business fell into a pattern. The large firms like Siemens & Halske supplied equipment to the municipal utilities on credit, receiving securities in return. The manufacturer then sold the securities at a profit. If everything turned out satisfactorily, the electrical equipment manufacturer earned its first profit with the delivery of the equipment, then an additional profit from the sale of the securities. The manufacturer frequently profited also from the operation of the newly erected power plants. Not all suppliers, of course, were in full command of such a complicated and risky financing business. Heavy losses forced many enterprises to submit to the control of banks or to merge with other, mostly larger, partners.[31]

Construction and financing of electric streetcar systems followed a similar pattern. Siemens & Halske delayed entering the business of supplying the electric streetcar industry until its engineer Walter Reichel devised a slightly arched sliding shoe to pick up power from an overhead trolley wire. Although Siemens had displayed an electric streetcar as early as the world exhibition in Paris in 1881, the firm had to wait for Reichel's innovation before it could enter the business in 1889. After 1889 investments in public local transportation increased rapidly.[32] In 1891 there were electric streetcar lines in 3 German cities; in 1896 42 streetcar lines operated on 582 kilometers of track. By 1903 electric local public transportation extended across a total of 3,692 kilometers of track in 134 cities.[33]

The Siemens brothers also expended considerable effort to obtain foreign sales of their electric railways. They demonstrated electric railways in operation at the International Electrical Exhibition in Paris in 1881, as we have mentioned, and at the All-Russian Industrial Exhibition in 1882, but without any immediate return in business. In the 1880s the firm commissioned and built just three streetcar systems. In 1882 Siemens & Halske constructed a line between Mödling and Vorderbühl for the Austrian Southern Railway Association (Österreichische Südbahn-Gesellschaft), and in the same year a line between Frankfurt and Offenbach in Germany for the Weinmann Bank. In 1883 the company won a contract for a system in Portrush, Ireland.

Siemens & Halske as a rule was reluctant to serve as general contractor for the construction of electric power plants. The risks involved in such projects were high, and the firm had only a comparatively minor share of the necessary products. In addition, any such endeavors would tie up a considerable amount of the firm's financial resources. Werner von Siemens opposed founding a company of his own for the construction

International Electrical Exhibition, Paris, 1881

of central power stations. Primarily, he desired to be the builder of these plants and the manufacturer of the necessary machines and equipment, but not himself be engaged as an investor. His reluctance allowed other firms, more willing to accept the risks involved, to enter the business.[34] In the hectic development that took place during the 1890s, which was characterized by a massive oversubscription of stock issues, more big corporations came into existence: Union-Elektrizitäts-Gesellschaft, a subsidiary of the Thomson-Houston Company; Helios AG, a public corporation, formerly the O. L. Kummer Company, and the Electricitäts-Actien-Gesellschaft W. Lahmeyer & Co. At the end of the nineteenth century a total of seven such enterprises existed in Germany.[35]

With the relatively small capital base of a family enterprise, Werner von Siemens was in the 1880s not in a position to compete successfully on the capital market with a public corporation such as Rathenau's DEG (later AEG).[36] In this situation, moreover, the technical lead enjoyed by his enterprise over rival firms and his personal high reputation as an authority in electrical engineering were of no use.

Business via Representatives and Agencies

Although fundamental modifications of the entire organization of the Siemens enterprise were carried out after the turn of the century, the marketing system had to be adapted to the growth of the firm much earlier. The firm's marketing system reflected the company's stage of development. During the first decades of Siemens & Halske's existence, there was no reason for the firm to establish any external sales organization, since for its main product—telegraphs—business was conducted with public authorities, which maintained direct contacts with the company. As long as the number of customers was relatively small, centralization of all domestic marketing in Berlin was perfectly feasible. Even when telegraph sales increased, the market structure of a small circle of customers did not change fundamentally. Even the largest telegraph projects were planned and executed by dealing with national authorities and administrations. (This structure has remained valid for key fields of communications technology up to the present day.) Only when electric power technology developed and expanded was the firm forced to decentralize its marketing efforts. Lacking its own organization, Siemens initially had to cooperate with qualified partners. Outside of telegraphy, the business procedures had to be adjusted to deal with the considerably more numerous private customers. Not until the second half of the 1870s did Siemens & Halske employ its first sales representatives for its products in Germany and abroad.

After the reorganization of the enterprise in 1868, Werner von Siemens had to envisage a new marketing policy. The expansion of the business and the much wider manufacturing program made it impossible to secure a sufficient volume of orders solely by means of the personal efforts and contacts of Werner and his brothers, as had been the case with the supply of telegraph lines and equipment during the first years. With the entry into the age of electric power, establishing a marketing organization became mandatory.

After the company had expanded well beyond telegraphy,

Siemens authorized representatives to handle the sale of electric generators and arc lamps. Later it authorized representatives to arrange the installation of complete generating plants. The members of the family, however, reserved for themselves any negotiations with governmental authorities, as well as the entire low-current business. The representatives chosen were usually engineers residing in the respective cities. Some of the representatives were former telegraph engineers who had shifted their professional efforts toward the new field of electric power technology and had established engineering offices. Their main task was to sell generators and electric arc lamps, and eventually also to install complete lighting systems based on incandescent lamps. Only occasionally, and then only after extended negotiations with Siemens & Halske, did the representatives handle the sale of products from other divisions of the enterprise, for example, the sale of articles and systems of low-current technology.

Initially, the network of representatives covered mainly the German Reich, but it soon included other European countries as well. The network abroad was never very dense, however. In a listing dated March 2, 1880, in addition to the firms in St. Petersburg, London, Paris, and Vienna, Siemens & Halske representatives abroad were listed only for Rome, Zurich, Brussels, and The Hague.[37] The relationship between these representatives and the home office in Berlin was not always smooth. A main concern for Werner von Siemens was finding qualified persons, sufficiently knowledgeable in the technology involved to be able to supply dependable expert advice. Preferably, a representative abroad would also be capable of taking care of the installation and maintenance of plants. Such a representative should accordingly have an engineering office in his territory and, if at all possible, be an expert in electrical technology. The farther away the marketing territory was from Berlin, the more the representative had to meet these demands. Werner von Siemens was not afraid to reject applicants if they did not meet his expectations. Thus he wrote during the negotiations over an agency in Japan in 1884:

In general the scope of our production is too diversified and too complicated for a general agency to be successful in a country far away. Many attempts in this respect have turned out to be failures. Our products are not direct trade articles, the sale of which concludes the business. To introduce our products, technical knowledge is essential. This requirement cannot be replaced by mere instruction. In order to recommend our products convincingly, thorough understanding of their advantages is paramount, i.e., total command of the respective field. . . . Only an engineering firm—perhaps and at best in combination with a commercial one—would be able to represent us successfully.[38]

Werner von Siemens realized that one of his firm's most valuable assets was its reputation. A sound reputation, he believed, was both an effective advertisement and a means to future contracts. An incompetent agent would not be able to offer the tailor-made solution, which Siemens & Halske always promised its customers. If in doubt, for the sake of the high quality of their products and of their good reputation, it was preferable to do without some agencies, even if this resulted in the loss of business. The nature of this decision was as fundamental as had been the maxim of the early years to compete successfully on the basis not of low prices but of good quality.

In exchange for its high expectations of its representatives, Siemens & Halske did not offer much. The agents had to work at their own risk. The firm neither took on warranties they had entered nor did it offer any support. Goods were manufactured and shipped on secure orders only. The buyer had to pay all expenses for freight and insurance from the factory in Berlin. The agent was granted a commission of 10% on the gross amount of the order, which was not due until payment of the amount specified in the invoice. The agents were obliged to exclusively sell products made by Siemens & Halske. This was a sound arrangement from the standpoint of the company's management, because it meant that the firm had to negotiate with only a few customers and bookkeeping requirements were minimal.

From another standpoint, however, this method of doing business was very disadvantageous, because Siemens & Halske relinquished direct control of all customer districts. Consequently, bills receivable started to pile up at the agencies, which sometimes had a narrow financial base. The risks associated with the customers were thus largely unsecured. From the technical standpoint in particular, marketing via agencies was unfavorable. As Siemens & Halske was not engaged in the installation of the products delivered, there was no way to find out how the products stood up to stress and strain when in operation, whether there were any defects or deficiencies, what types of troubles occurred, and so on.

The marketing system based upon agents soon failed to cope with the highly diversified operations of the company. As early as 1885, the management of Siemens & Halske saw the need to upgrade the agency business. Technical offices established by the firm itself were seen as offering considerable advantages. Management recognized the need to approach the customers with the intention not merely of making a quick sale but also of offering consulting and planning services. In order to implement this new strategy, it was necessary to maintain bases as close to the customer as possible. It was hoped that this marketing configuration would enable Siemens & Halske to approach the customer very early on, in order both to shape the projects according to the firm's concepts and practices and to win the subsequent orders.[39]

Since the agents at home and abroad were in no way integrated into the management structure of the enterprise, they almost inevitably got into conflicts of interest with the firm. They differed from the members of the Siemens family or long-term employees, who had, preceding the gradual expansion of the agency network, negotiated and executed sizable contracts, in that these agents were not bound either by family ties or by other loyalties to Werner von Siemens's marketing concept. Since the agents worked on their own account, they would frequently buy materials for installation and other accessories not from Siemens & Halske itself but from less expensive suppliers—to the annoyance of Siemens & Halske.

As Werner von Siemens had taken great care to ensure a stable relationship between the firm on the one hand and its key executives and its workers on the other hand, his total disregard for this aspect of the business during the gradual expansion of the sales force comes as a surprise. Up to 1885 the terms of the contracts with the sales representatives were not even standardized. In 1885 uniform guidelines were defined, but deviations from these standards were frequent, particularly in the case of foreign business. Thus, a special contract was in effect for Edouard Rau, the representative for Belgium, which Rau had concluded for a period of ten years after long bickering.[40]

The Rau case in particular illustrates the specific difficulties arising from this type of agency business. Since 1871 Rau had worked for Siemens & Halske without any formal contract and had occasionally negotiated and concluded contracts, often with a highly fluctuating volume of sales. According to his own evaluation of his activities, Rau had been working primarily out of an interest in electrical-technical products and out of his high personal esteem for Werner von Siemens. He therefore took offense at the request to formalize the relationship by means of a contract. In a letter dated January 24, 1882, he wrote to the top management of Siemens & Halske:

> Certain conditions in business life develop and modulate themselves according to the persons and circumstances involved. Among them are some that fit less easily than others into everyday commercial legal forms. This also applies to the relationship I have had the honor to maintain with you, and if my character had not suited you, and if I had not for years engaged in your business without any profits but more as a hobby, a way of life that my financial means fortunately allowed, we would not even be in a position today to hunt for the forms into which we now want to squeeze ourselves.[41]

The contract Rau finally agreed upon, guaranteeing him the sole franchise for Belgium, the safeguarding of the patent rights there, and a commission of 10%, but allowing no special deviations, was not able to soothe the irritations that had grown between the parent firm and its representative. After the contract expired in 1892, the parties separated in a mood of general disagreement.

Even when dealing with long-term employees Werner von Siemens adamantly refused to make concessions. For example, in 1890 he was not willing to grant Carlo Moleschott, who together with various partners had been Siemens & Halske's representative in Italy since 1881, a fixed monthly salary or other special terms to tide him over a temporarily tight financial situation. In a letter written in a very friendly tone, Werner von Siemens plainly stated that Moleschott could get better results only with higher sales. Paying the representatives a fixed monthly salary would not benefit Siemens & Halske.[42]

On the one hand the reluctance to assume any share of the expenses the marketing outlets incurred, and on the other hand the inefficiency of the central management in monitoring the representatives, particularly those abroad, resulted in a generally poor business climate. Customers' complaints about unsatisfactory installation of equipment were regular causes for quarrels between the Berlin parent firm and its representatives. If a plant completed and put into service subsequently caused trouble, frequently the result was mutual recriminations between Siemens & Halske and the representative. While the representatives blamed the malfunctions on deficiencies in the material supplied, the officers in Berlin argued that the execution of the installation at the site was faulty. Consequently, in several cases customers were only willing to sign contracts directly with the parent firm in Berlin. In such cases the representatives naturally felt cheated out of their commission. Even the "General Guidelines for Representatives" ("Allgemeine Vertretervorschriften") set up in 1885 did not result in the basic improvement of the situation or in a change in the conduct of business.

Compared to that of the Siemens enterprise, the marketing organizations of its competitors, which rapidly gained ground, were much more elaborate and aggressive. At a very early stage, the Nuremberg firm S. Schuckert & Co., for example, started to develop a marketing organization fully integrated with the enterprise. For a short period, DEG had made use of Siemens & Halske's marketing facilities, but in the middle of the 1880s it started to establish its own technical offices under the management of Felix Deutsch. This development was expanded after the founding of AEG: the firm established a cost intensive yet functional distribution and maintenance network abroad. The same was true for American rival firms, which also pursued much more effective marketing strategies. Thomson-Houston and Westinghouse spent large sums on marketing structures with strong regional dispersion.[43]

Not until the 1890s, after Werner von Siemens's withdrawal from the top management, did Siemens & Halske make substantial efforts to create a marketing network fully integrated with the enterprise. The second stage in the expansion of marketing was characterized by the gradual discontinuing of business with independent agencies, by the direct hiring of reliable people, and by developing the firm's own sales centers, called Technical Offices (Technische Büros). These external marketing offices, which were staffed with engineers, were to watch for sales opportunities and to clarify the prerequisites for solving problems, to such an extent that subsequent processing and managing of projects could be handled by the parent firm at home. Over time, the simpler offers were prepared directly by the Technical Offices themselves.[44] The earlier agencies, which had only negotiated contracts, were thus replaced by competent technical advisers. This feature was also emphasized by the term *technical office*.

The spread of Siemens & Halske's Technical Offices proceeded slowly. Back in the autumn of 1879 the company had established the Vienna Technical Office of Siemens & Halske Berlin, but the only thing this branch had in common with the later Technical Offices was its name; it represented the nucleus of what eventually became the factory of Siemens & Halske in Vienna. (A few years later, at the beginning of the 1880s, the term technical office was dropped from the name of the Vienna establishment.) The first real branch office in Vienna, in the true sense of the term technical office, was established in 1890 by the local factory works. The structure of this branch was similar to that of the municipal office of the Schuckert firm in Nuremberg; it was intended to relieve the factory from the small business of installations and the sale of parts. On January 20, 1890, the first Technical Office Siemens & Halske was established in Munich. A short time later a second Technical Office was established in Mulhouse, Alsace, followed by offices in Cologne, Hagen, Frankfurt, and Dresden. Starting in 1894, the transportation department was placed in charge of the entire marketing system of the electric power business. Before the turn of the century, the Vienna factory also established the first Technical Offices in other parts of Austria, eventually totaling twenty-one branch offices in 1914.[45] However, owing to its slow start in establishing the Technical Offices, Siemens & Halske lost its leading market position in the Austro-Hungarian Empire.

Production Abroad

Generally speaking, business firms that emphasized research and technical progress founded production firms in other nations as part of the last stage of their development of an international orientation and strategy. Siemens & Halske was an exception to this general pattern of business development. As we have seen, Siemens & Halske became an international firm, albeit one with kinship ties closely intermixed with business activities, before it developed its own marketing organization. London was its outpost for production abroad, where, after the acquisition of the factory in Woolwich, Siemens & Halske began to operate its own production facilities in 1863.[46] After the expansion of the cable factory in Woolwich in 1873 and the acquisition of a gutta-percha processing factory, production in England increased continuously. Nevertheless, the British branch of the firm still acquired many devices and parts from Berlin, a practice that continued even after Werner and his brothers in effect dropped the concept of the comprehensive enterprise and founded Siemens Brothers & Co. Ltd. on January 1, 1881. Time and again Berlin and London argued

Siemens factory, Hainburgstraße, Vienna, 1890

over the special terms to be granted. In its main field of activity, however—the production and laying of submarine cables—the London firm grew independently.

The situation changed in Vienna when the company began local production there in 1883. Before that time the Vienna branch had operated only as a workshop for repair jobs and the installation of equipment. But when the Vienna branch was awarded large orders in the field of railway safety, orders substantially exceeding the manufacturing capacity of the facilities in Berlin, execution of these orders was shifted to Vienna. Shortly afterward, the scope of production in Vienna was expanded to include electric generators and arc lamps. The construction of three central electric power stations, which Siemens & Halske subsequently operated on its own account while also providing the administration, increased the business of electric lighting to such an extent that the facilities were enlarged in 1887. Following Werner von Siemens's retirement in 1889–90, a second factory had to be established to accommodate the production of lead-shielded cables. The production facilities and the administrative offices were grouped into two separate units, with Vienna I taking care of production while Vienna II handled project management and the administration of the electric power plants.[47] The Vienna office was also important for the sale of electric streetcars.

Business with Russia reached a new peak after Carl Siemens returned to St. Petersburg in 1880. In spite of poor business there during the 1870s, Siemens & Halske had remained the market leader, yet in the new field of electric illumination it had to face the competitors Yablochkov and AEG. After the All-Russian Industrial Exhibition in 1882, Siemens & Halske constructed a cable factory in Russia. As in the case of the establishment of cable production in Berlin, this was done in order to qualify for a large order that was supposed to be granted to a firm with domestic production in Russia. This Russian facility also allowed the firm to avoid the high import tariffs that had been levied in 1877. The cable factory formed the nucleus of the later United Cable Factories St. Petersburg, which was run jointly by Siemens, AEG, and Felten &

Siemens factory, St. Petersburg, built 1882–83

Guilleaume. The successful completion of such highly presti-
gious illumination projects as the floodlighting of the wide,
luxurious boulevard Nevsky Prospekt in 1884 and of the Winter Palace made the demand for central electric power stations
in Russia rise by leaps and bounds. Initially, Siemens & Halske
was unwilling to assume responsibility for the generation of
electricity but only prepared to supply the necessary machines.
In February 1887, however, Carl Siemens, acting for the
Siemens's St. Petersburg business, which had been independent
from the parent firm in Berlin since 1880, became a partner in
the new Company for Electrical Lighting (Gesellschaft für
Elektrische Beleuchtung), which had a capital of 1 million
rubles and, according to the regulations spelled out in the license, was authorized to lay power cables and construct central electric power stations in all parts of Russia. This
partnership paid off well in the years to come: from 1904 until
1911 Siemens made huge profits from the shipments of three-
phase turbogenerators to Russia. For the time being, however,
there was another downtrend in business, even causing Carl in
1890 to try—unsuccessfully—to sell the St. Petersburg business at an acceptable price.

The last project Werner von Siemens started before his death was the establishment of a branch of his enterprise in the United States. In 1886 Werner had authorized the German American Henry Villard to market his patents, especially his patent on lead-shielded cables, for Siemens & Halske in the United States. He envisioned either an outright sale of the patent or a partnership in a company already operating. As the president of the Edison Electric Light Company, Henry Villard, together with Georg Siemens, the director of the Deutsche Bank in Germany, prepared to proceed toward a substantial financial interest of the German electrotechnical industry in the Edison General Electric Company, which had resulted from the merger of the various Edison companies in 1889. Along with AEG and the Deutsche Bank, Siemens & Halske bought shares of 1 million marks, mainly with the intention of starting the production of lead-shielded cables in the United States. Werner explained this in a letter dated January 21, 1890, to Henry Villard: "We subscribed to the tune of one million marks not out of hope for profits from a rise of the price of the stock, but only in order to secure and accelerate the implementation of the planned contract and the construction of the cable factory according to our system."[48]

The development of the American venture proceeded slowly, however. Negotiations on the contract to use Siemens technology in a new factory for lead-shielded cables were protracted. Apart from the production of lead-shielded cables, Werner von Siemens was also interested in entering the American market with his electric railways and streetcars, but patent litigation involving several American railway construction companies prevented a quick entry into this market as well. All plans had to be scrapped when, in 1892, the Edison General Electric Company merged with the Thomson-Houston Group to become the General Electric Company. The president of Thomson-Houston unequivocally took charge in this merger, and the banks forced Henry Villard to withdraw from the new General Electric Company. As a consequence, the German investors rapidly backtracked.

Nonetheless, Siemens & Halske executives remained interested in penetrating the American electric streetcar market, and they decided to pursue the matter on their own initiative. In January 1892 Werner's oldest son, Arnold, traveled to the United States, initially intending to sell his father's patents. After making inquiries, however, Arnold Siemens changed course and investigated establishing a company of his own that would include production facilities. Consequently, on March 4, 1892, Siemens & Halske, together with two American partners, O. W. Meysenburg and A. W. Wright, founded the Siemens & Halske Electric Company of America, located in Chicago, Illinois. They specified the purpose of the enterprise as the production and sale of electric generators, railway motors, and associated equipment. At first the new firm was successful, receiving numerous orders, but a devastating fire completely destroyed the factory, abruptly snuffing out the company's transatlantic hopes. Damage amounted to $600,000; production was never restarted.[49]

The "Private Business" in the Caucasus

Werner von Siemens ran a "private business," the copper mine at Kedabeg in the Caucasus Mountains, in addition to his enterprises in the electrical industry. Werner had bought the mine, together with his brothers Carl and Walter, in 1864. The purchase upset Halske, who thought the risks involved were not worth the additional work. Even after Halske's withdrawal from Siemens & Halske, the Siemens brothers exempted Kedabeg from the legal contracts between them. The Kedabeg copper mine also remained a constant source of annoyance for those associated with Siemens who did not participate in the venture.

Werner bought the mine because he thought it would be a good project for Walter to supervise. The mine, which had rich deposits, was in bad condition, yet Werner thought Walter could turn it into a profitable venture. Walter knew the Caucasus. Stationed in St. Petersburg, he had supervised the

The copper mine at Kedabeg in the Caucasus Mountains, ca. 1865

construction and the maintenance of telegraph lines in the Caucasus for his brother Carl. In the course of those activities, Carl had discovered the mine with its rich deposits of copper. Carl and Werner also developed a growing interest in the project.

After the death of his first wife, Mathilde, Werner von Siemens made his first trip to the Caucasus. Two more visits were to follow. On his first journey he inspected the mine and detected two main drawbacks: its remoteness and the logistical problems this caused, and the low professional skill of the employees. Above all, the poor infrastructure of Transcaucasia turned out to be a crucial problem. Between Kedabeg, situated near Elisavetpol, and the Black Sea—a distance of about 600 kilometers—there was no railway or hard-surface road. All materials and equipment for the operation of a modern mine had to be imported from Europe and transported to the mine site. The second problem concerned the workforce. The nomadic population of the area was willing to work in the mine only until they had accumulated enough money to meet the necessities of daily life for awhile. Consequently, there was no long-term stable workforce. For this reason, Werner von Siemens suggested trying to settle the workmen permanently in the vicinity of the site by building solid masonry homes for them and their families, which might motivate them to accept long-term employment and to work on a regular schedule. The key positions at the Kedabeg mine were filled by German officials and by Russians from the Baltic provinces.[50]

When Walter Siemens suffered a fatal accident in the summer of 1868, Werner von Siemens traveled to the Caucasus for the second time. Walter's death left a vacancy in the management of the mine (and also at the German consulate in Tbilisi, where he had served) that turned out to be particularly difficult to fill. Nevertheless, the mine continued to operate quite profitably, and the Russian government offered more mine projects to the brothers.

Carl had initiated improvements in metallurgical technology at the mine. He would have welcomed an opportunity to continue to manage the mine, but his active management proved impractical. At first Werner had thought the brothers would integrate the mining activities in the Caucasus into their comprehensive enterprise, but this did not happen. The profits from Kedabeg were never more than about 20% of the profits made in Berlin or London, although the mine's returns were rising. Nevertheless, Wilhelm Siemens, as the administrator of Walter's estate, urged his brothers to concentrate on more-important activities.[51] Eventually, however, it was not Wilhelm's admonition but his wife's ill health and eventual death that influenced Carl's decision to dedicate himself primarily to the electrical side of the family business and to move to London.

Werner believed it essential that a member of the family represent the Siemens firm in Tbilisi to ensure that an outbreak of "business anarchy" (*geschäftliche Anarchie*) did not occur.[52] Werner urged his youngest brother, Otto, to obtain the appointment as German consul in Tbilisi and to look after the mine's affairs. Otto, who suffered from tuberculosis, had already spent some time with his brothers in Tbilisi and was well acquainted with the business situation there. Otto's experience and physical strength, however, were not sufficient for the management of the mine. So Carl, while living in London, continued to manage Kedabeg.

Carl had little luck with the directors employed at Kedabeg. In 1871 the situation improved slightly when Otto, by marrying Annette von Krehmer, widow of Prince Swiatobolk-Mirski, gained considerably more influence in Tbilisi. The improvement in the mine's operation proved short-lived, however, because Otto fell victim to his illness in the autumn of 1871. Without the direct supervision of one of the Siemens brothers, the director of the mine in the 1870s, Carl Schnabel, ran it down. In his final report on Kedabeg in 1876, Carl Siemens wrote that Schnabel had been ill for half a year but had done the least damage to the firm during that period of time.[53] Schnabel's successor, Gustav Kölle, turned out to be more suitable; he stayed in Kedabeg until 1905. Under his direction the copper production of the mine soon increased greatly, and after 1877 the mine was profitable. Werner von Siemens remained interested in this enterprise, even though it differed substantially from his other activities. When in 1890 he wrote about his trips to the Caucasus in his memoirs, he was still contemplating plans for the modernization and reorganization of the mine, which he wanted to see developed and expanded into a European model plant.

5

Werner von Siemens's Conception of Himself as a Businessman

Siemens as a Family Business

Werner von Siemens's family orientation was one of his most striking characteristics as a businessman. Numerous self-portrayals substantiate not only that his preference was to plan and conduct his business operations with members of the family, but also that concern for his family's well-being was the primary motivating force in his business career.[1] Werner von Siemens initially used the term *family* to refer to his brothers and sisters; in later years, *family* referred above all to his children. Werner relied less on other relatives, such as his cousins Louis and Georg or his more distant relatives, the nephews Georg and Alexander. He regarded them rather as an "ultimate reserve in case of an emergency."

The need to take care of his family was the decisive factor in Werner's decision to become a businessman. Werner von Siemens himself declared his family as the guideline for his business activities in a letter written to his brother Carl at Christmas 1887: "As a matter of fact, you have always put much more emphasis on the real goods in life than I, who have

132

chased after far too many phantoms and ideas. . . . I think that in business the object of making money is only in second place; it is for me rather an empire which I have founded and which I want to leave to my descendants undiminished, so they can continue being active in it."[2] The employment of members of the family, moreover, opened up the chance to put competent and loyal coworkers into remote and important positions abroad. Yet in the course of time and in the face of the growing emancipation of the brothers, more and more problems popped up that could only with great difficulty be patched over by brotherly love.

Following Halske's withdrawal from the enterprise, it was, apart from some minor portions of the capital, totally in the hands of the brothers. Werner thought the time was ripe to implement his idea of an extensive "comprehensive business," and he anchored this idea in contracts. Without an explicit formal statement, he claimed for the parent firm in Berlin and for himself, as the senior manager and head of the family, the top position. But with the planning of the Indo-European telegraph line and with the laying of the first submarine cables, the London branch had expanded to equal the parent firm in Berlin with respect to importance, volume of business, and profits. His brother Wilhelm, a naturalized Englishman by that time, had also developed into an established figure in technology and was no longer willing to take second place to his older brother.

According to his brother Carl, Wilhelm had increasingly developed into a "very irksome associate."[3] Along with this, there were two reasons for quarrels. First of all, London was no longer willing to accept without question instructions from the Berlin parent firm. Moreover, Löffler, who held power of attorney, believed that the prices of Berlin's products were too high. Löffler directed the London firm to engage other suppliers or to request special terms, which Berlin was not willing to grant.

Wilhelm did not care much about these business problems, yet he backed Löffler and in his correspondence with Berlin often displayed an undertone of annoyance. According to the testimony of Carl Siemens, the vanities of the two "Dr. W. Siemens" worsened the atmosphere. Occasionally they were mistaken for each other in the press, and inventions of one brother were sometimes credited to the other.[4]

For himself, Werner claimed—probably with justification—that he always treated his brothers in a very conciliatory fashion. In the contracts about the comprehensive enterprise, Carl and Wilhelm were allocated high proportions of the profits, even though Werner by far held most of the capital. In addition, the telegraph business mainly exploited Werner's patents. Wilhelm and Carl were granted a share in the factory producing the alcohol meters and received proportional shares of the return paid on the capital and of the dividends distributed from that part of the business. The factory in Charlottenburg, which was to be run by their cousin Louis Siemens, promised to be very profitable owing to the great demand from Russia. This financial padding enabled Wilhelm and Carl to pursue their usually unprofitable pet projects. For a time, with his brother Friedrich, Wilhelm constructed steel furnaces and ran a steel plant in Landore, England, which, while being technically interesting, only incurred losses. Carl had started other unsuccessful enterprises in Russia, including a sawmill and a glass factory.

In return for his financial generosity, Werner expected the brothers to accept his idea of a comprehensive enterprise to be run under his management from Berlin. With Carl's help, who had less difficulty acknowledging his elder brother, this basic concept of running a business was formally maintained up to 1880. The reorganization undertaken in 1880 had several causes: Carl's return to Russia, Wilhelm's progressive withdrawal from the common business, and finally Werner's desire to integrate his sons into the enterprise.

Altogether Werner had six children. His first wife, Mathilde, had borne four children: two sons, Arnold (b. 1853) and Wilhelm (b. 1855), and two daughters, Anna (b. 1858) and Käthe (b. 1861). He had another daughter, Hertha (b. 1870), and a son, Carl Friedrich (b. 1872), with his second wife, Antonie Siemens, the daughter of a distant relative, whom he married four years after Mathilde's death. Werner was eager to have his sons succeed him and was very pleased when the two eldest sons, Arnold and Wilhelm, joined the firm. He wanted them to participate early as partners, sharing the responsibility as well as the profits. In this respect his situation was different from that of his brothers: Wilhelm did not have any children, and Carl's son, Werner, was not much interested in business or technology and also was of poor health. The new partnership agreement, dated December 28, 1880, consequently spelled out only the general willingness of the partners to agree in principle with the entry of Werner's sons, Carl's son, and "a person of Wilhelm's confidence" into the business at a later stage, if they should so desire. In the event, Werner's first two sons were integrated into the firm as partners: Arnold on January 1, 1882, and Wilhelm on April 25, 1884.

The agreement also sealed the separation of the London firm from the Berlin parent firm. The common administration of capital remained the only link between the public company Siemens Brothers & Co. Ltd. in London and the parent enterprise in Berlin. While Werner, as the chairman of the association of shareholders, had some general supervisory authority, the London management had to be granted extended authority in the conduct of business, not least because of the great distance between the two firms. The firm in London was managed by Ludwig Löffler, who, after Wilhelm's death in 1883, was largely unsupervised by any member of the family. Wilhelm picked as his successor his distant nephew Alexander Siemens, who was loyal toward Berlin and to his uncle Werner von Siemens but was not in a position or willing to assert himself against Löffler as the managing director.

The first subject of dispute was the calculation of the internal prices for products supplied from Berlin to London. Löffler had always felt these prices were too high, and he had reproached Berlin officials while the comprehensive enterprise still existed. Much more serious, however, than those irksome quarrels was the second subject of dispute: the rivalry between the Berlin and London firms over the world market after the dissolution of the comprehensive enterprise. This long-term dispute between Werner von Siemens and Ludwig Löffler came to be called the "Löffler crisis." Although the conflict of interests had been brewing since the 1860s, it had always been resolved more or less amicably among the Siemens brothers; but in 1883 the conflict broke out openly. The partnership agreement of 1880 stipulated that the two firms would not compete with each other on the world market. Löffler interpreted this term to mean that the total overseas market was to be within the sphere of interest of his London enterprise, basing his claim on a special passage in the articles of incorporation of the family stock corporation. (There is no record of such a passage.) The parent enterprise in Berlin, however, wanted to restrict Siemens Brothers Ltd. to Britain and the British colonies. It would have been disastrous for Siemens & Halske in Berlin to have to refer all overseas customers to the London firm. London charged prices far above those of Berlin, and allowing London the entire overseas market would probably have caused potential customers to switch to rival firms.[5] In an embittered tone, Werner von Siemens commented on this attempt to limit the activities of the Berlin parent firm in a letter to his brother Carl: "I would prefer to withdraw right now as one of the executive managers of the Berlin business than to sign a contract that would condemn the parent firm, the very essence of my activities, to future infirmity by tying off its vital arteries. The motherly love that Berlin has always extended toward its children must, if necessary, have its limits."[6]

The solution to this problem was made more difficult by Löffler, who, while not being a member of the family, was nevertheless a shareholder in Siemens Brothers Ltd. Although he had initially held only a few shares, by the end of 1886— thanks to clever purchases from other officials—he had enlarged his holding to a blocking minority of more than 25% of the total number of outstanding shares. In this way he was able to prevent his own dismissal. Löffler's strong minority stake also gave him some leverage in trying to persuade Werner von Siemens to accede to his demands. Siemens & Halske reacted by filing a lawsuit against Löffler. Siemens Brothers retorted by filing a countersuit, based on "continuous, unlawful competition on the world market" ("fortgesetzte, unrechtmäßige Konkurrenz auf dem Weltmarkt").[7]

Werner and Carl could have used their power as majority stockholders in Siemens Brothers Ltd. to have the lawsuit withdrawn, but they decided not to do so because of the English legal system. Instead, they settled the dispute with Löffler out of court. Löffler agreed to sell all his shares to Werner von Siemens. Based on the contract, he was to sell 600 shares immediately to Werner at £85 a share, and 625 additional shares no later than January 1891 at the same price. Löffler was entitled to receive dividends until the date of the actual sale. He was to sell the remaining 28 shares to Alexander Siemens.

This prolonged quarrel with London had grave consequences. While the electrical industry experienced a worldwide boom and rival firms rapidly expanded with the help of the newly created banking network, the further advancement of Siemens & Halske on the world market was considerably delayed. Since the London firm was primarily responsible for the cable business, Siemens quickly fell behind rival firms as new markets for electric power technology opened. Until Werner von Siemens's withdrawal from active business, the overseas markets remained unexploited by Siemens & Halske.

The Löffler crisis was not an isolated case, although it had the most negative consequences. There were also difficulties with cousin Louis Siemens, who was a partner in the Charlottenburg factory. As a result, the brothers were eager to terminate their agreement with him even before the contract expired in 1885.

Although having the legal status of a public company or including more members in the corporation would have offered possibilities for a considerable expansion of the equity capital, Werner von Siemens stuck to the "family principle" (*Familienprinzip*).[8] Nevertheless, he thought it best to guard his own interests. Following the bad experience with London, Werner even preferred to have the formal right to end the collaboration with his brother Carl, with whom he had always been on good terms. In the last partnership agreement, intended to specify the organizational structure of the enterprise after his withdrawal, Werner was concerned above all with securing unlimited authority for his sons in Berlin. In a letter he pleaded for Carl's understanding:

> So it will be Berlin, which I have always imagined to be the hereditary seat for my sons. You cannot imagine how happy I am to have two sons who are competent and who are called to continue the business after our deaths, and a third son seems to be developing well in the same direction. At all events, I wish to leave them the business under conditions that ensure a secure continuation. There are two prerequisites to be met. First, all inheritance rights per proxy must be excluded from management and capital regulations, and second, there must not be any interested people who might be able to request liquidation. For this reason I have supported a paragraph authorizing each of us, after the expiration of the partnership agreement, to request to take over the business he is conducting solely on his own account and to compensate the other partners by paying them the book value of their portion of the business.[9]

At the same time, however, he reassured his brother that neither he himself nor his sons would plan to exclude Carl from the top management of the Berlin firm in the future. Indeed, Arnold and Wilhelm asked their uncle to come to Berlin as senior executive immediately after Werner von Siemens's death.

This patriarchal attitude with respect to legal details concerning the operation of the firm and its staff policy is astonishing in a man who called himself a liberal. His strong sense of the family kept the businessman, who in other respects was so farsighted, from initiating important reforms and contributed to the "stoppable rise of AEG" ("aufhaltsamen Aufstieg der AEG").[10] Quarrels such as the Löffler crisis prevented the firm from keeping up with the worldwide expansion of German electrical technology, which it otherwise could easily have done. Because of the business policies it adopted, Siemens fell behind its competitors. Werner's sons, however, were able to catch up after they took over management of the firm.

Werner von Siemens, 1892

In his later years Werner von Siemens was very reluctant to give up his dominant position in the firm. The limited partnership agreement dated December 27, 1889, spelling out his withdrawal as a partner and his rejoining the firm as limited partner on January 1, 1890, conceded him numerous rights. He secured himself the right to be consulted on essential decisions, such as the purchase and sale of real estate and companies, the founding of new branches, the conclusion of business deals exceeding a value of 100,000 marks, and the hiring or dismissal of top managers. In addition, he continued to be authorized to take part in business meetings and to have unlimited access to all files and correspondence. His was to be, at best, a semiretirement. As a visible sign of his integration in the firm, Werner kept his office and could still use the services of

Siemens employees for his private accounting and correspondence.[11] These rights were expressly limited to Werner
himself and did not apply to his heirs. His sons Arnold and
Wilhelm, the top managers of the firm, rose to full power only
after his death.

The Company's Social Policy

Werner von Siemens was paternalistic in his relationships with
his employees as well. He tried hard to fill the key positions of
his enterprise with persons dependably loyal to him because of
family ties or close friendship. Of course, he did have to work
with employees or workmen with whom he had no personal
relationship. Influenced by the shortage of skilled workmen,
particularly in times of full order books, Werner early on pon-
dered the question of how to motivate and bind his employees
to the firm.[12] He also felt morally obligated not only to pay employees their wages but also to let them have a share in the
profits, which in his view all employees had earned. He wrote
to his brother Carl: "The money earned would burn like a red-
hot iron in my hand if I did not give the faithful employees
their expected share. It would also be imprudent of us if they
ended up with no reward for success at moments of great new
endeavors."[13]

Thus Werner instituted a system of profit sharing as the
most promising way to reward key officials, who bore a great
deal of responsibility.[14] The circle of such "participants in the
profits" (*Tantiemisten*) always stayed very small,[15] but minor
officials also received bonuses. Not only did Werner von Siemens feel obligated to share some of the profits with the
workforce, he also recognized that the company itself would
benefit if the goals of employees and those of management coincided. As he noted to Carl:

> I have always found it most wasteful if those who participate
> in the management of the firm do not also participate in the
> results. If a single silly mistake can be avoided by such an

investment, the benefit for the enterprise may far exceed the amount paid out as a bonus! In the face of large business operations and complex deals impossible to monitor all the time and manage personally in every detail, we have to pass on a major part of the profit to our deputies. This is a basic rule for effectively conducting big business operations! Ever since all masters in the shops in Berlin have gotten an annual award, proportional to the profit each individual shop earned, quite a new spirit has entered our enterprise; we produce more, at lower cost and of better quality, and cannot cope with the amount of work.[16]

From an early stage in the history of the Berlin workshop, Werner von Siemens looked after his staff well, a policy that assured continuity in the workforce and avoided a shortage of skilled workers. After 1855 he rewarded employees at Christmas according to individual performance and the profits of the business. Moreover, Werner von Siemens endeavored to establish a good personal relationship with his workmen. Until sometime after 1870, each year he invited all master craftsmen and officials to his house on Ascension Day for personal talks in order to learn more about their needs and problems. Over time, however, the enormous growth of the enterprise and the transition from craftsman-dominated manufacturing to "factory-style" production made such personal contacts increasingly difficult to maintain. The employees had to be motivated in a different way. This was done by introducing piecework wages, which quickly enabled the workers to earn much higher wages than before. At the same time, Werner was farsighted enough to recognize the greater stress the workers experienced doing piecework and reacted by reducing the working hours. After 1872 the workers at Siemens & Halske had to work only nine hours a day (fifty-four hours per week). Despite the considerable rise in actual wages, the firm reaped some benefits also: the cost of the products dropped after the introduction of the piecework system. Nevertheless, the older members of the workforce, oriented toward craftsmanship, accepted the piecework system reluctantly.

The introduction of a pension fund in 1872 on the occasion

of the firm's twenty-fifth anniversary represented an outstanding step forward in social policy. This fund was devised to provide retirement benefits for the workers and to bind younger employees to the firm, especially important since after the 1870s, with the introduction of the free choice of work and the right of assembly, the mobility of workers had increased considerably throughout the economy. The fund, which was started with 50,000 thalers donated by the three Siemens brothers and 10,000 thalers by Halske, served to increase the loyalty of the majority of the employees—those who were not paid bonuses and for whom management did not consider profit sharing to be appropriate. Werner von Siemens had considered establishing such a fund as early as 1868 for all branches of the enterprise and wrote to his brother Carl: "At any rate we have also to establish a pension fund for the Tbilisi business [copper mine and smelting plant]. I think we should establish a big one for all branches, to which the different business operations and the people themselves pay contributions. Please give this some serious thought. By the way, Halske and I have always considered the reserve fund as a means of binding the people to our firm, not only those who receive awards."[17] The donation of 60,000 thalers provided the foundation for the pension fund for cases of old age or disability. Moreover, Siemens pledged to pay an annual contribution for each worker and official to the fund's financial administration, elected by the participants. After uninterrupted employment of thirty years, workers were entitled to draw a pension amounting to two-thirds of their wages. The fund also provided support for widows and orphans. The claims were forfeited only if the employee resigned. If workers had to be dismissed because of a lack of orders, they received a certificate entitling them to reemployment as soon as the order situation improved.

The pension system was popular. Many workers kept on working, even when they drew pensions after thirty years of service, and regarded the pension as an additional source of income and a reassuring safety net. The attachment of the workers to the enterprise was greatly increased by this fund, all the more so as they did not have to contribute to it themselves, in

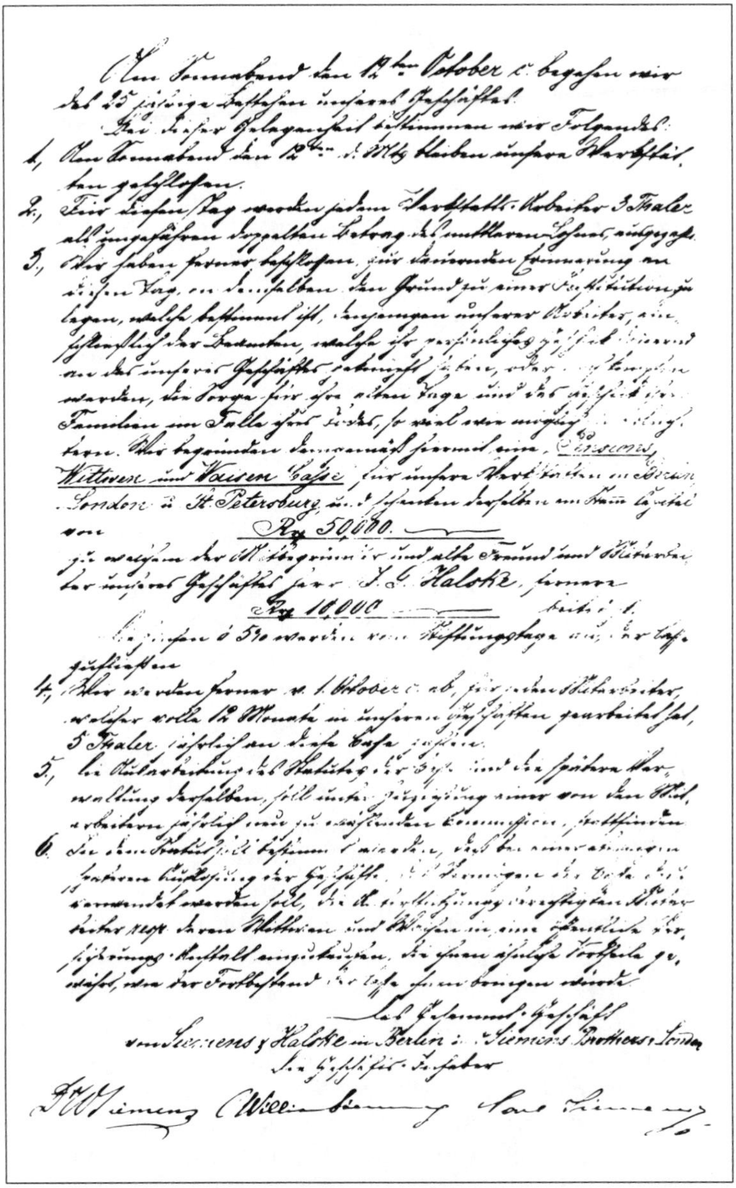

Charter trust deed for the pension fund, October 21, 1872

contrast to the national old-age and disability insurance system, which became obligatory in 1889. Since the firm's pension fund was an internal arrangement of the enterprise, it was
unaffected by the national pension scheme.

In his social policy Werner von Siemens, for rational reasons, suppressed his otherwise strong patriarchal inclinations.
The desire to interfere in the private affairs of his workers in
the "attitude of a benevolent country squire"—which can be
seen in the case of Alfred Krupp, for example—cannot be attributed to Werner von Siemens. Anxious to avoid having such
a neopatriarchal grip on his labor force, he abstained from
building company-owned housing, despite the difficult housing conditions in Berlin. As early as 1883, plans for building
such housing had been discussed at Siemens & Halske, but
they were never approved.[18]

The attitude adopted by Werner von Siemens was characterized by his conviction that social conflicts had to be solved
on the basis of mutual concessions, since all persons working
in a company were dependent on one another. When negotiat-
ing with his workers, time and again his healthy egoism enabled him, on the one hand, to find ways and means to meet
their legitimate claims and, on the other hand, to refuse to
agree to anything that, in his opinion, could harm the firm and
thus also the gainful employment of the workers.

In his memoirs Werner von Siemens stated his motivation
for providing such social benefits to his workers: "At an early
period of my life I had already recognized that a satisfactory
development of the continually growing firm was achievable
only if a happy cooperation of all employees based on their
own initiative for the advancement of their interests could be
secured. In order to reach this aim, I thought it necessary to
have all members of the firm participate in the profits according to their individual performance."[19] The recognition that
his employees' satisfaction with their work coincided directly
with his own fundamental interest combined harmoniously
with his philanthropic and caring disposition. There was another side of the coin, however: Werner von Siemens expected
his employees to be absolutely loyal and to strictly maintain in-

dustrial peace.[20] If there were any conflicts, they were to be solved exclusively internally and without the participation of outsiders. Violations of the hierarchical structure of the firm were severely punished, up to dismissal—a style of management characterized as "liberal patriarchalism" (*liberaler Patriarchalismus*) by Jürgen Kocka, a term that at first glance appears contradictory but means something like benevolent patriarchalism. Unlike in the United States and Great Britain, in Germany large manufacturers such as Siemens did not face well-organized labor unions. Not until 1918, just after the end of World War I, did German law accept unions.

On the managerial level Werner von Siemens continued to favor close informal contacts instead of strict contractual regulations. As the enterprise grew, he particularly regretted losing contact with middle management. The top management, of course, remained in the hand of the family and close friends.

Werner von Siemens's Political Position

As the bulk of his time was taken up by his activities as a businessman, scientist, and inventor, Werner von Siemens was unable to dedicate himself to politics for extended periods. He was politically active only during short spans of his life, concentrating on specific issues that attracted his interest. He never perceived himself as a politician or a lobbyist.

Most likely Werner von Siemens's political attitude was strongly influenced by his liberal parents, with later modifications resulting from his contacts with the Prussian state. As we have seen, there were numerous indications during his military service of his basic liberal attitude, the most significant of which being his enthusiastic welcome of the revolution of 1848. However, as Werner was dependent on the Prussian state and later on the particularly reactionary Russia as customers, in regard for his business interests he kept his distance from revolutionaries. Considering that Werner von

Siemens was investigated several times for political reasons before his entry into Russia, this attitude becomes all the more understandable.

Werner von Siemens began his actual political activity in the 1860s, although his firm was still growing and thus facing financial and organizational problems. In 1860 he joined the National Union (Nationalverein). Following the model of the Italian Societa Nazionale, liberals and democrats had joined in this party in order to support the idea of a unified Germany. The more Prussia turned toward a nonconstitutional policy following the beginning of the so-called new era under King Wilhelm I, the more difficult the position of the National Union became.

Werner von Siemens adopted a position distinctly in opposition to the Prussian government when in 1861 he established contacts with representatives of the Prussian Landtag (state parliament) interested in founding a new liberal party primarily in opposition to the Prussian military reform initiated by Albrecht Graf von Roon, the secretary of the army. In his memoirs Werner von Siemens claimed credit for having had a decisive influence on the naming of this new party. The representative Hermann Schulze-Delitzsch is said to have proposed calling the party the German party (Deutsche Partei). Werner, however, suggested the Progressive party (Fortschrittspartei). As a compromise, it was decided to found the German Progressive party (Deutsche Fortschrittspartei).

The German Progressive party was highly successful in the parliamentary elections of December 1861; with 109 representatives, it constituted the strongest faction in the Landtag. Together with the left-of-center representatives, the party was in a position to block the passage of the government's plans for a reform of the army. The king reacted by dismissing the liberal ministers and dissolving the chamber in March 1862.

For the new elections, Werner von Siemens was persuaded by his friends in the party to be a candidate for the constituency of Lennep-Solingen. The triumph of the German Progressive party, which won 230 out of a total of 352 seats, also procured a seat for Werner von Siemens in the Landtag, allowing him to follow an opposition course in the "question about the army." At the peak of the fight over the proposals concerning the budget and enlarging of the army, he wrote to his wife on June 10, 1863: "I am determined not to put up with anything at all, come hell or high water. If Prussia remains as it is for a long time, I am not inclined to pay it the honor of my presence much longer."[21]

Werner von Siemens's stance was characteristic of the changing attitude of so many German liberals. Bismarck's military successes made him uneasy, and particularly the victory in the Austro-Prussian War of 1866 caused a change in his mood, which is evident in a letter to his brother Wilhelm dating from September 1866: "I am deeply convinced now of Bismarck's being moved by the Holy Spirit of a grand national mission, to be resolved not to create a half-sized Germany only, but a whole nation. This is the reason why I have detached myself from most of my former political friends and have campaigned and voted for the vote of confidence in his foreign policy, since he stated that he would consider the approval of the state loan. This should, however, now mark the end of my political career, at least for the time being. I will hold myself accountable to my voters and at the same time resign from my mandate."[22] For this reason Werner supported the reconciliation between parliament and the government. A bill of indemnity, which granted the government retroactive approval for the expenditures between 1862 and 1865 which had not been approved by the parliament, ultimately rendered this reconciliation possible.

The German Progressive party experienced a crisis after the Battle of Sadowa (Königgrätz). In the elections in July 1866 the party suffered a heavy defeat. In autumn a group split away and formed the nucleus for the National Liberal party. This party successfully sought to be on good terms with Bismarck in the future North German Reichstag. Werner von Siemens did not run as a candidate for the future Landtag or Reichstag.

Werner was not the only liberal making his peace with Bismarck after 1866. Great parts of the German middle class acted similarly and withdrew from politics, placing all their hopes on Bismarck. In retrospect, Werner von Siemens regretted his decision, recognizing that the ruling landowners had consolidated their political position under Bismarck.

Werner von Siemens withdrew from politics in 1866, not only because of the crisis in the Prussian liberal movement but also because of an argument with his constituency. Disagreements arose with the factory owners there about their duty to identify German products as "made in Germany" and also about protective tariffs. Werner von Siemens strongly supported the marking of German products as German instead of providing them with English seals, as was common at that time. In doing so he also saw an important contribution toward developing pride among German factory owners. Nor did he want to get roped in as a lobbyist for protective tariffs, because he estimated their effects to be mostly negative:

> An effective protective tariff system, which for industry secures consumption in its own country, can only operate effectively if this country, as, for example, the United States of America, contains all climates and produces all the raw materials required for its industry. Such a country can lock itself against any import, while simultaneously, however, reducing its own export capability. It must be regarded as a stroke of luck for Europe that America, because of her prohibitive protective tariff system, has impeded the dangerous, rapid development of her industry and reduced her export capabilities.[23]

Such profound differences of opinion with the factory owners of his constituency, who were clamoring for the introduction of protective tariffs, facilitated Werner von Siemens's decision to resign from his mandate as a representative in the Prussian Landtag. Looking back, this former supporter of the opposition who had changed sides to become a national-liberal follower of Bismarck had some trouble explaining and justifying his earlier attitude. In his memoirs Werner also had difficulty in putting his disapproval of the increase in the Prussian military budget into a favorable light. Indeed, his opposition in the 1860s had for a long time forfeited him King (later

Kaiser) Wilhelm I's favor. On an official occasion Wilhelm is said to have disclaimed in a gruff tone any knowledge about a Lieutenant Siemens. Accordingly, not until the liberal-minded emperor Friedrich III had succeeded Wilhelm I was Werner von Siemens raised to hereditary nobility, in 1888.

Werner von Siemens did not completely withdraw from politics after he abandoned his second candidacy and converted from an opposition supporter to a man mostly favoring Bismarck's politics. Sometimes he was called upon to lend his expertise to help solve special problems. Werner also continued to be involved in public policies that were of special interest to him. In particular, the reorganization of patent legislation was close to his heart, and he devoted much energy to it after the Franco-Prussian War of 1870–71. Prussia granted patents at the discretion of civil servants for a period of three years at most. In general, patents had to be applied for in each individual member state of the German Tariff Union (Deutscher Zollverein). Consequently, inventors tried to market their inventions in England, France, or the United States first—that is, in countries where their rights to a patent were substantially more comprehensively protected.

As early as 1863 Werner von Siemens composed an expert opinion on the protection of patents for the Berlin Chamber of Commerce, in whose Council of Elders he had been active since 1855. In order to accelerate action on this matter he organized the Society for the Protection of Patents, which he chaired, and persuaded some lawyers to join the association. This society prepared a draft for a law specifying the following regulations: each invention filed should first be examined to determine the originality of the basic idea, and descriptions of the invention should be prepared for display in places accessible to the public. Patents granted should be published in full; protection of a patent should extend over a period of fifteen years, with fees, rising incrementally every year, levied for this protection. A patent court should be created and empowered to void previously granted patents. In his memoirs Werner von Siemens emphasized that the proposal was by no means contradictory to his convictions on free trade, as the protection for a patent would inherently be tied to the immediate and complete description and publication of the invention. The government of the Reich did not react immediately on the patent society's proposal. In a petition to the chancellor of the Reich (*Reichskanzler,* a position similar to that of a prime minister), Werner von Siemens pointed out the poor reputation of German products abroad, which were regarded as cheap and of low quality, and stressed that improved protection of patents might remedy matters. In a reaction to this petition, the unified German state passed a new patent law in 1876, which was a slightly modified version of the draft submitted earlier by the Society for the Protection of Patents.

With the passing of the new patent law, Werner von Siemens had for the first time successfully influenced politics as a lobbyist. To a great extent he continued to take part in this area, becoming a member of the Patent Office of the Reich following the passing of the National Patent Law (*Reichspatentgesetz*) of 1876. In connection with this position, to his great amusement he was given the title of privy councillor (*Geheimer Regierungsrat*). In his memoirs Werner gave this title a poor rating, contrasting it with his pride in the scientific distinctions and honors granted to him during his life. Among these honors were the authorization to present lectures to the French Academy of Sciences, bestowed in 1850; an honorable doctorate from the philosophical faculty of the University of Berlin in 1860; and admission into the Royal Academy of Sciences in Berlin in 1874.

Consonant with his scientific interests, Werner exerted his political influence to promote the education of a new generation of engineers. This was one of his principal concerns. In 1879 he had participated in the foundation of the Electrotechnical Society (Elektrotechnischer Verein), under the leadership of Heinrich von Stephan, the postmaster general of the German Reich. The society had two main goals. It sought to establish a system for the definition of units for such electrical properties as voltage, current, and resistance; and it promoted the establishment of chairs for professors in electrical engineering at the technical universities.

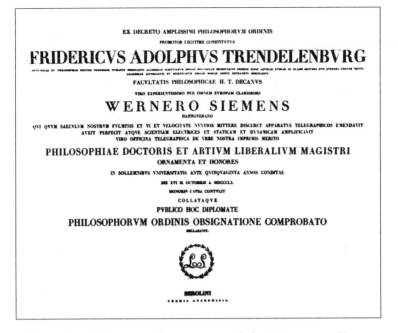

EX DECRETO AMPLISSIMI PHILOSOPHORVM ORDINIS

PROMOTOR LEGITIME CONSTITVTVS

FRIDERICVS ADOLPHVS TRENDELENBVRG

FACVLTATIS PHILOSOPHICAE H. T. DECANVS

VIRO EXPERIENTISSIMO PER OMNEM EVROPAM CLARISSIMO

WERNERO SIEMENS

HANNOVERANO

QVI QVVM SAECVLVM NOSTRVM FVLMINIS ET VI ET VELOCITATE NVNTIOS MITTERE DISCERET APPARATVS TELEGRAPHICOS EMENDAVIT AVXIT PERFECIT ATQVE SCIENTIAM ELECTRICES ET STATICAM ET DYNAMICAM AMPLIFICAVIT VIRO OFFICINA TELEGRAPHICA DE VRBE NOSTRA IMPRIMIS MERITO

PHILOSOPHIAE DOCTORIS ET ARTIVM LIBERALIVM MAGISTRI

ORNAMENTA ET HONORES

IN SOLLEMNIBVS VNIVERSITATIS ANTE QVINQVAGINTA ANNOS CONDITAE

DIE XVI M. OCTOBRIS A. MDCCCLX

HONORIS CAVSA CONTVLIT

COLLATAQVE

PVBLICO HOC DIPLOMATE

PHILOSOPHORVM ORDINIS OBSIGNATIONE COMPROBATO

DECLARAVIT.

BEROLINI

FORMIS ACADEMICIS

Diploma for the honorary doctorate awarded to Werner von Siemens in 1860

Moreover, Werner von Siemens also supported the foundation of an institute devoted solely to research and not intended for teaching. He was ready to engage himself in such a project not only as a politician promoting science but also as a sponsor. For this purpose he had intended to put into his will an endowment for the promotion of scientific research, but he decided to offer the government before his death a site for the erection of such an institute of the Reich (*Reichsanstalt*). The Reich would then assume the cost of the building and the expenses for the support of the institute. Accordingly, in 1885 an agreement was concluded with the government, and the Physikalisch-Technische Reichsanstalt was founded in the district of Charlottenburg in Berlin on a site donated by Siemens.

As a man engaged in politics, Werner von Siemens showed himself to be totally "a product of his time." At first he was very enthusiastic about the revolution of 1848, yet kept a distance from the "deep red party" ("blutrote Partei") and soon dissociated himself from revolutionary ideas. During the liberal atmosphere of the new era and during the Prussian constitutional conflict, he became involved and had his most active political period. Following Bismarck's successes in the military field and in foreign policy, and after the foundation of the Reich in 1871, he changed into a supporter of the government and was only occasionally critical in private. The political influence he exercised as a successful industrialist was directed totally toward the solution of factual problems in which he had a personal interest. His comments in his memoirs on the future role of Europe have lost none of their relevance, even a century after his death: "If Europe wants to maintain its dominant position in the world or at least stay equal to America, it must prepare itself in time for this struggle. This is only possible by removing all of the inner-European customs barriers, which limit the market, make production more expensive, and diminish competitiveness on the world market."[24]

6

Further Expansion of the Siemens Concern: 1890 to World War I

Siemens Goes Public

In the last decade of the nineteenth century, the management structure of Siemens & Halske began to change. The change was in response to the altered conditions of the electrical industry. The company underwent a major management reorganization under the influence of the Deutsche Bank. Werner von Siemens's retirement and death freed the company to undergo such a transformation. In spite of his outstanding technical talents and his general business acumen, Werner had never fully grasped the changes occurring in the nature of his industry, especially the importance of competition from giant rivals such as AEG, and had been reluctant to accept changes in the corporate form of his enterprise. The company did, however, begin a change in its legal form in 1890, as we have seen, a change that was completed in 1897. This reorganization of Siemens & Halske was an indication that the firm had reoriented its strategy.[1]

Even earlier, at Wilhelm's suggestion, the London firm had been converted into a public corporation in 1881. Also, the St.

153

Petersburg Society for Electrical Lighting was founded as a public corporation in 1886.[2] Then, effective January 1, 1890, the former ordinary partnership Siemens & Halske was converted into a limited partnership, the assets of which were estimated at 14 million marks. Carl Siemens and Werner's sons Arnold and Wilhelm were the personally liable partners (the owners of the business), while Werner remained a limited partner with a capital contribution of 6.2 million marks.

Although Werner von Siemens died a wealthy man, his estate and the capital of the firm that bore his name proved insufficient to meet the needs of the business in the 1890s. In his will Werner von Siemens had specified the transfer of his portion of the capital of the enterprise to his six children in equal parts. Besides the three liable partners, the limited partnership was made up of five limited partners with a total capital contribution of 12 million marks. The total contribution of the three liable partners to the firm's capital was at least as great as the capital contributed by the limited partnership. Accordingly, the firm had a capital of at least 24 million marks at its disposal when Werner died. In the electrotechnical industry, however, the demand for capital rose considerably, particularly in years when the organization of corporations and contractor enterprises, following the example set by AEG, was rapidly increasing. As early as October of 1892 Siemens & Halske had to take out a loan of 10 million marks at an interest rate of 4.5%, secured by a mortgage—the first money drawn from external sources since the founding of the firm.[3]

Siemens & Halske finally became a public corporation in 1897, albeit one in which members of the Siemens family were firmly in control. The conversion into a public corporation was finally triggered by the plans of Emil Rathenau to merge AEG and the Union-Elektrizitäts-Gesellschaft. For Siemens & Halske, such a merger would have meant the loss of support from all the large banks in Berlin.[4] Formally, the founding of the Siemens & Halske Corporation took place on June 3, 1897, effective as of August 1, 1896, by transferring all assets and liabilities of the limited partnership Siemens & Halske to the new corporation against shares worth 28 million marks.

Additional shares at a par value of 7 million marks were taken over by members of the Siemens family, who thus held all the stock of the corporation. In order to secure the ironclad influence of the family, and against the opposition of the Deutsche Bank and its director, Georg Siemens, the details of the corporate charter were written in such a way as to permit effective exclusion of any major outside influence.[5] In paragraph 22 the charter of the corporation granted the supervisory board rather sweeping rights and invested it with full authority in paragraph 25: "At any time the chairman of the supervisory board is authorized to monitor the entire conduct of business of the board of management and will accordingly have access to all books and correspondence of the company. The supervisory board is also entitled to transfer the execution of the aforementioned authority as well as other specific assignments to members of the supervisory board and other persons outside of the management and to specify the applicable remunerations."[6] This regulation was entered into a draft granting a "delegation of the supervisory board" (*Delegation des Aufsichtsrates*) far-reaching authority.[7] Despite reservations expressed in bank circles, the statutes of the new company were set up so as to maintain the earlier influence of the liable partners in the new legal form of the enterprise.

There were further provisions for ensuring the family's continuing control of the corporation. According to paragraph 20 of the charter, the corporation's board of management was subject to the instructions of the supervisory board. According to paragraph 27 the supervisory board was authorized to transfer the execution of its authority onto individual members, in reality onto the chairman of the supervisory board, who acted as the "chief of the House" (*Chef des Hauses*) and guaranteed the uniform conduct of the Siemens concern. The basic principles of these regulations remained unchanged until a revision of the charter required by a new German law of 1937 spelling out the rules for corporations. These regulations were undoubtedly in accordance with the family's interests; yet the intended cementing of the influence of the family made a rapid increase of the capital stock of the firm more difficult.[8]

The Founding of Siemens-Schuckertwerke Ltd.

The German electrical industry began to be concentrated into the hands of a few firms in 1901 and 1902. Siemens and AEG emerged from this process as the dominant firms in the industry.[9] Enterprises in financial straits were either taken over by AEG or Siemens or jointly liquidated by the two large companies in order to eliminate competition and increase their dominance of the market. When the Union-Elektrizitäts-Gesellschaft and the Elektrizitätsgesellschaft vorm. S. Schuckert & Co. met with difficulties in 1902, Schuckert & Co. entered into negotiations with AEG but eventually merged with Siemens & Halske.[10] Siemens & Halske transferred its own activities in the field of electric power into the newly founded Siemens-Schuckertwerke Ltd.[11]

Siemens undertook this merger rather unwillingly, and agreed to it only to prevent the further growth of AEG.[12] Siemens-Schuckertwerke (SSW) Ltd., founded in 1903, integrated all the activities in the field of electric power of the Siemens Corporation and the Nürnberger Elektrizitäts-AG vorm. Schuckert & Co. (Nuremberg Electricity Corporation, the former Schuckert & Co.) founded earlier by Sigmund Schuckert, which dominated a substantial part of the market, above all in Bavaria. Schuckert's cash balance had risen from 20.3 to 136.5 million marks between 1893 and 1900/01, yet the firm had not been able to secure the commensurate financial backing. Its internal financial base was relatively small, and when the firm was hit by a crisis it could not count on sufficient support from the smaller banks in southern Germany. Part of the difficulties probably also arose from the fact that Schuckert's director general, Alexander Wacker, was not paid a fixed salary. Wacker theoretically received 15% of the net profit, but his share was reduced by an allocation to the statutory reserve fund and the payment of interest on the stock of the company. In effect, then, he received only 4% of the net profit. With this in mind, Wacker obviously was interested in disbursing large profits. Between 1893 and 1902 Schuckert had distributed dividends amounting to 19,479 million marks and additionally distributed 5,313 million marks in dividends from means made available by the capital market. In order to secure future access to the capital market, the dividends were continuously increased in order to demonstrate the soundness of the enterprise.

Financial considerations precluded a full merger, which would have been the most logical course. The integration was reduced to a partial one, which resulted in Siemens & Halske's having control of the majority of the stock. Schuckert was transformed into a pure holding company.[13] Despite the separation of the fields of production, the production of incandescent lamps remained with Siemens & Halske. The same was true of the department in charge of constructing Berlin's elevated railway and subway system, which later developed into a branch company of its own.[14] Siemens was ready to cooperate with AEG in certain fields, but no longer was it willing to leave the field to its most dangerous competitor without a fight.[15] By pooling all its own divisions in the field of electric power with Schuckert to form Siemens-Schuckertwerke Ltd., the Siemens concern, which through Siemens & Halske had had ever since its founding a leading position in the market in low-current technology, also advanced into a strong position in areas where AEG was principally active.[16] The result was that Siemens became almost equal to Emil Rathenau's enterprise, even though substantial funds had to be invested during the first years. Within the Siemens concern, Siemens & Halske Corporation and Siemens-Schuckertwerke occupied the position of core companies. The capital of Siemens-Schuckertwerke Ltd. amounted to 90 million marks, split almost equally between Siemens & Halske and Schuckert, with Siemens & Halske's share exceeding Schuckert's by 100,000 marks—to have a clear definition who was the boss in case of disagreement in matters involving the centralized management of the enterprise. Siemens & Halske and Siemens-Schuckertwerke Ltd. were actually directed by a common management, even as they legally remained two independent companies.[17] By founding Siemens-Schuckertwerke and through the ensuing transfer of the electric power business, Siemens &

Halske Corporation became a mixture of a manufacturing and holding company, although it considered itself rather a "technical holding company."[18]

Although in terms of sales or assets Siemens and AEG were almost of equal ranking during the last years before World War I, there were important differences between them. Each firm exhibited characteristic features indicating their different management policies. Whereas AEG had indisputable priority in the field of electric power technology and in the contractor business, Siemens dominated low-current technology and played a leading, if not dominant, role in the field of electric power. Siemens focused on activities involving electricity and before World War I avoided excursions into nonelectric technology (the sole exception was its starting to produce automobiles in 1906). In this regard the firm continued to follow Werner von Siemens's original principle of being active in the entire field of electrical technology. Siemens & Halske dealt with all kinds of communication—whether via cables or overhead lines, or wireless (radio)—and with measuring technology. It also produced cables and insulated wires for communication technology.

Time and again new fields of research and production developed from this wide range of activity, as the firm was able to utilize the results and the experiences collected in one field in the promotion and refinement of another. Innovations such as high-speed telegraphy, simultaneous transmission of several telegrams via a single line, telex, direct dialing telephone systems, telephone communication via cables, access to the precise time via telephone, radio technology, and sound in movies were all in some way associated with the name Siemens & Halske.

For their part, Siemens-Schuckertwerke produced generators, electric motors, and transformers; manufactured switchgear and switchgear plants; and constructed and commissioned entire power plants. Its scope of production included accessories and components for electrical installations; incandescent lamps; lighting systems for cities, households, and factories; motors and associated equipment for farms, mining, industry, households, and heating appliances; and cables and circuits for electric power.[19]

Even after the change in its legal status to that of a limited company, Siemens stuck to the system of self-financing typical of a family-run enterprise, while AEG frequently tapped the capital market. The stock of the Siemens & Halske Corporation, which had been augmented in 1900, was not raised again till 1909. The funds acquired via loans during the nineteenth century lasted until 1912. New financial means obtained in 1909 and 1912 were required primarily by the financial needs of SSW Ltd., as the initial capital of 90 million marks remained unchanged and SSW Ltd. had, owing to its legal structure, no easy access to the capital market. Consequently, most of the investments made by SSW were also self-financed. Starting in 1906/07 the dormant reserves, which were already considerable, were increased enormously by the practice of fully writing off the machines and instruments in the year of their purchase. This cautious way of financing, which can be traced back to the founder and was still practiced a century after his death, preferred safeguarding a long-term liquidity in contrast to aiming for optimal profitability. On December 27, 1910, Wilhelm von Siemens commented on the Siemens & Halske balance of 1909/10: "About 6 to 7 million again to be added to the dormant reserve, at a dividend of 12% . . . SSW about 5–6 million entered into the dormant reserve."[20]

This financial policy served Siemens well during Germany's difficult years between World War I and World War II. The financial caution exercised by Siemens proved decisive in helping the firm gain and hold a strong competitive position and a high level of technical progress. For the remainder of the twentieth century, thanks to its management's financial caution, Siemens performed better as a business, overall, than did German competitors that preferred riskier ways of financing and that assumed those risks in order to diversify into nonelectrical fields.[21]

The foundation laid by Werner von Siemens served his family, his company, and the electrical industry well. By 1914, when World War I broke out and German and European history experienced a turning point, the essential elements of electric power technology and electronic communications were known, were well under development, and had found wide application. Electrical energy turned out to be the least expensive and most versatile and efficient form of energy. New areas for the use of electrical energy were opening almost daily during the first decades of the twentieth century. Among the different forms of energy, electrical energy had gained the leading position because it was easy to transport in large quantities and over long distances and could be converted conveniently and efficiently into other forms of energy. In the field of power technology, all kinds of machines were known and being used in a variety of specialized applications. The demand for electrical energy had enormously increased since the introduction of the incandescent light and the growth in the demand for electrical motors. After the turn of the century, a particularly intensive development was initiated by the use of individual electrical motors in industry, above all in mining and in heavy industry. The ratings of the electric power stations continually increased. After the turn of the century the process of linking individual power stations into power grids began. Within a decade the power of the electrical machines increased from less than 100 horsepower at the beginning of the 1880s to 1,000 horsepower and to more than 5,000 kilowatts after the turn of the century. In this way even before World War I the electrical industry had outgrown its initial role in the production of machines providing mechanical energy without exhaust gases or refuse, in the production of equipment for lighting, and in communications. Developing equipment and devices to control and regulate industrial processes and sequences by means of electricity, the industry had developed into an indispensable supplier of an ever increasing variety and quantity of equipment for other industrial branches. The Siemens companies substantially contributed to this growth of electrical technology and of the German electrical industry. The work of Werner von Siemens as an inventor and as a businessman was bearing great fruit.

Appendix

Tables

Table 1. Workforce and Sales, 1848–1870

Year	Total Workforce	House of Siemens Workforce	Sales (1,000 M)	Export Sales (1,000 M)	Profits (M)
1848	18	18	10.3	5	
1849	28	28	58.1	41	45,000
1850	49	49	221.8	272	96,000
1851	50	50	253.1	132	?
1852	90	90	514.0	447	10,414
1853	49	49	212.8	693	13,500
1854	130	90	594.9	323	17,282
1855	268	122	801.1	293	142,988
1856	332	119	466.0	367	60,600
1857	367	127	470.3	408	61,700
1858	408	166	563.7	375	108,700
1859	419	174	509.2	280	73,400
1860	401	180	462.9	175	73,100
1861	438	181	381.5	256	27,100
1862	492	175	351.2	192	21,000
1863	515	198	456.8	383	26,700
1864	660	193	589.7	269	83,300
1865	652	135	670.1	277	133,300
1866	733	166	621.5	210	189,200
1867	672	192	685.1	467	142,000
1868	691	211	900.4	507	243,900
1869	836	271	1,052.0		397,900
1870	1,080	380	1,543.0		475,170

Note: The data on workforce and sales differ considerably in the Siemens archive documents. The data given here, which are based on the Z-report, dated May 16, 1966, are officially considered valid.

161

Table 2. Workforce, 1847–1892

Year	Siemens & Halske	Siemens & Halske Vienna	Gesco	Siemens Brothers	Russia	Total
1847						
1848		18				18
1849		28				28
1850		49				49
1851	50					50
1852	90					90
1853	49					49
1854	90				40	130
1855	122				146	213
1856	119				213	332
1857	127				240	367
1858	146	20		2	240	408
1859	154	20		10	235	419
1860	150	30		23	198	401
1861	141	40		40	217	438
1862	135	40		50	267	492
1863	168	30		50	267	515
1864	163	30		200	267	660
1865	135			250	267	652
1866	166			300	267	733
1867	192			350	130	672
1868	211			400	80	691
1869	271			450	115	836
1870	380			550	150	1,080
1871	446			850	90	1,386
1872	581			900	110	1,591
1873	558		70	934	110	1,672
1874	540		110	1,601	100	2,351
1875	499		72	458	90	1,119
1876	469		161	239	90	959
1877	698		40	461	130	1,329
1878	729		94	348	140	1,311
1879	635	2	117	1,254	120	2,128
1880	631	6	239	495	120	1,491
1881	675	10	220	1,418	130	2,453
1882	725	27	333	765	140	1,990
1883	899	68	333	856	170	2,326
1884	1,026	109	302	1,735	200	3,372
1885	1,142	120	306	963	220	2,751
1886	1,258	105	259	738	240	2,600
1887	1,361	320	397	687	260	3,025
1888	1,722	373	354	699	330	3,478
1889	2,125	688	271	1,019	410	4,513
1890	2,737	1,041	172	1,065	530	5,545
1891	3,057	1,127	178	990	590	5,942
1892	3,325	1,199	251	1,118	640	6,533

Source: SAA 29/Le 932.

Note: Figures differ slightly in the various archive files. Therefore they sometimes do not add up to the total.

Table 3. Sales by Division, 1847–1874 (in thalers)

Year	Total Sales			Foreign Sales			Export Quota (%)
	Telegraphy	Water Meters	Total	Telegraphy	Water Meters	Total	
1847	74		74				0.0
1848	3,420		3,420	21		21	0.6
1849	19,379		19,379	1,470		1,470	7.6
1850	73,949		73,949	1,546		1,546	2.1
1851	84,281	70	84,351	13,431	70	13,501	16.0
1852	170,315	835	171,150	89,849	835	90,684	53.0
1853	70,760	165	70,926	43,856	135	43,992	62.0
1854	198,293		198,293	148,977		148,977	75.1
1855	267,030		267,030	230,842		230,842	86.5
1856	155,325		155,325	107,665		107,665	69.3
1857	156,756		156,756	97,687		97,687	62.3
1858	181,891	6,069	187,961	122,108	258	122,366	65.1
1859	162,543	7,182	169,725	135,022	918	135,942	80.1
1860	149,952	4,177	154,130	124,102	859	124,961	81.1
1861	121,304	5,838	127,142	92,805	474	93,279	73.4
1862	107,929	9,132	117,062	56,704	1,752	58,456	49.9
1863	141,941	10,169	152,111	83,196	2,030	85,226	56.0
1864	186,332	10,171	196,503	62,175	1,799	63,974	32.6
1865	200,211	22,399	222,610	120,117	7,403	127,520	57.3
1866	177,419	17,229	194,649	86,711	2,871	89,583	46.0
1867	206,044	19,482	225,526	86,174	6,112	92,287	40.9
1868	252,006	26,883	278,889	62,925	6,967	69,892	25.1
1869	311,889	33,217	345,107	144,465	11,125	155,590	45.1
1870	401,663	35,815	437,478	158,541	7,222	165,763	37.9
1871	445,166	83,932	529,098	130,502	11,041	141,543	26.8
1872	585,599	134,188	720,088	126,676	21,310	147,987	20.6
1873	620,416	150,063	770,479	114,853	13,287	128,141	16.6
1874	724,577	148,261	872,839	166,210	24,031	190,241	21.8

Source: SAA 29/Ld 893.
Note: See note to table 2.

Table 4. Sales by Region and Type of Product, 1847–1896 (in marks)

Region	Telegraphy	Incandescent Lamps	Water Meters	Dynamos	Cables
Germany	45,808,241	4,414,106	8,357,498	46,070,241	46,457,356
Sweden	250,012	212,149	32,050	1,975,403	1,041,185
Norway	204,975	12,057	12,108	119,564	47,863
Denmark	1,339,812	35,237	8,285	1,485,328	1,089,388
Holland	2,396,757	101,852	268,381	1,913,440	1,646,273
Belgium	1,166,987	37,400	1,267	271,659	109,707
Switzerland	441,352	229,497	496,846	2,261,300	674,032
Italy	236,582	252,017	126,235	3,262,542	1,170,118
England	2,527,456	279,835	211,211	870,124	84,136
France	307,706	150,498	6,401	1,005,516	480,906
Luxemburg	25,311	17,049	36,105	316,065	80,121
Austria	1,166,225	1,304,049	258,531	3,333,830	1,164,840
Russia	6,308,753	1,311,865	558,093	2,004,736	241,951
Spain	15,619	177,495	30,816	1,683,995	2,475,762
Turkey	110,114	189	42	85,599	44,377
Asia	71,596	76,517	2,410	804,663	149,551
Australia		59,413	65,820	23,376	24,212
Africa	13,952	1,662	131,351	3,900,178	812,673
Americas	372,074	124,035	61,330	3,623,214	427,609
Other countries	2,675	259,962	89,935	68,065	14,305
Total	62,766,208	9,058,595	10,754,726	75,078,848	58,237,041

Source: SAA 29/Ld 893.
Note: See note to table 2.

Table 5. Sales Distribution by Type of Product, 1867–1880 (in marks)

Year	Telegraphy	%	Water Meters	%	Dynamos	%	Cables	%	Other	Total Sales
1867	618,132	91	58,448	9						676,580
1868	756,018	90	80,650	10	5,654					842,332
1869	953,670	90	99,653	10	5,554					1,040,877
1870	1,204,990	92	107,481	8	14,482					1,326,998
1871	1,335,500	84	251,797	16	4,543					1,591,840
1872	1,757,699	81	402,566	19	6,896					2,167,161
1873	1,853,471	80	450,189	20	20,509				11,777	2,331,946
1874	2,165,905	83	444,786	17	17,391				7,832	2,635,910
1875	1,816,157	77	527,807	23	26,332				714	2,371,010
1876	1,659,135	79	367,674	18	66,171	3				2,092,980
1877	1,999,501	57	424,104	12	181,190	5	897,817	26		3,502,612
1878	1,885,032	41	584,568	13	484,027	10	1,636,267	13		4,589,894
1879	1,140,198	25	307,022	7	591,628	13	2,544,205	55		4,583,053
1880	1,257,740	20	315,931	5	826,636	13	3,985,727	62		6,386,034

Source: Waller, Studien, vol. 2, p. 55.
Note: See note to table 2.

Appendix

Table 6. Geographical Distribution of Sales,
1847–1872 and 1873–1897

Region	1847–1872 Sales in Thalers	%	1873–1897 Sales in Marks	%
Germany	8,846,858	55.0	163,373,003	69.2
Sweden	84,163	0.5	3,829,270	1.6
Norway	51,297	0.3	395,680	0.2
Denmark	386,642	2.4	4,547,490	1.9
Netherlands	268,162	1.7	6,947,912	2.9
Belgium	17,647	0.1	1,641,804	0.7
Switzerland	30,757	0.2	5,021,612	2.1
Italy	12,669	0.1	6,137,086	2.6
England	1,586,540	9.9	2,583,869	1.1
France	88,042	0.5	1,928,738	0.8
Luxemburg	3,988	0.03	588,897	0.2
Austria	240,173	1.5	7,789,428	3.3
Russia	4,122,163	25.6	8,395,463	3.6
Spain	3,241	0.02	6,347,546	2.7
Turkey	5,492	0.03	1,537,527	0.7
Asia	5,492		1,537,527	
Australia			209,938	0.1
Africa			8,249,742	3.5
Americas	12,662	0.08	6,739,078	2.9
Other countries			455,892	0.2
Total	16,092,915	100.0	235,977,429	100.0

Source: SAA 29/Ld 897 and 29/Lp 556.
Note: See note to table 2.

Table 7. Total Sales Accounted in Berlin, 1880–1896/97 (in 1,000 marks)

Year	Berlin Factory									Berlin Factory Total	Charlottenburg Factory						Total Sales
	Telegraphy	Telephones	Signals	Electro-chemical Equipment	Water Meters	Incandescent Lamps	Measuring Instruments	Dynamos	Cables		Dynamos	Cables	Siemens Brothers	Vienna I	Vienna II	Trains	
1880	824	88	310		361		61	835	3,953	6,466			467				6,933
1881	902	252	487		380		45	996	1,194	4,309			653				4,962
1882	824	297	477		353	4	38	1,327	379	3,794			992	56			4,841
1883	749	358	384		346	38	58	1,846	556	4,524			999	59			5,583
1884	796	374	429		342	43	70	2,140	661	4,858	339		896	381			6,473
1885	793	659	368		308	166	51	1,484		3,827	491	1,228	907	315			6,769
1886	667	826	352		404	493	46	1,879		4,668	325	1,005	777	332			7,109
1887	761	861	403		363	734	63	1,572		4,699	654	2,065	1,213	880			9,511
1888	969	1,259	314		453	667	69	1,628		5,358	1,318	2,386	1,105	839	437		11,443
1889	1,339	1,080	340		374	1,181	167			4,914	3,260	3,517	861	1,476	1,747		16,782
1890	1,279	1,080	415		372	1,133	153			4,842	5,161	6,514	548	3,378	3,057		23,788
1891	690	583	265		238	515	97	1		2,399	2,782	3,857	237	2,424	1,391		13,092
1892*	1,098	725	749	1	425	726	135	7		3,934	6,043	3,589	805	4,209	1,080		19,661
1892/93	852	413	501	1	445	589	150	8		3,053	5,224	3,275	830	4,321	1,197	231	18,131
1893/94	1,044	822	684	10	526	719	228	1		4,076	7,313	4,157	767	5,589	1,350	352	23,605
1894/95	1,151	436	721	18	358	857	313			4,120	10,261	4,933	872	7,739	1,145	2,541	31,612
1895/96	927	520	1,132	6	509	1,013	434			4,743	17,945	8,419	917	11,011	6,848	3,515	53,398
1896/97	983	866	1,706	15	495	913	438	16		4,490	20,480	8,105	1,246	9,197	1,885	3,689	50,913

Source: SAA 29/Lp 530.
Note: See note to table 2.
*Data for first half of 1892 only.

Table 8. "Remount" Accounts, 1856–1865 (in rubles)

Year	Expenditure	Income	Profits
1856	400,863	460,994	60,310
1857	325,450	423,645	98,194
1858	332,789	142,415	79,625
1859	388,225	511,727	123,502
1860	533,891	688,553	152,662
1861	318,802	443,385	124,582
1862	238,500	343,191	104,691
1863	323,904	419,364	95,460
1864	191,060	279,155	88,094
1865	171,771	269,751	97,979

Sources: SAA 17/Lm 184, 1 and 2, quoted from Kirchner, Deutsche Industrie, p. 47.

Table 9. Profits at Siemens Brothers, 1865–1880 (in pounds sterling)

Year	Profits	Year	Profits
1865	14,455	1890	88,570
1866	17,000	1891	33,977
1867	21,768	1892	24,461
1868	32,349	1893	-35,021
1869	25,822	1894	129,000
1870	69,005	1895	66,584
1871	30,504	1896	14,309
1872	-507	1897	19,690
1873	96,265	1898	18,339
1874	119,625	1899	22,769
1875	113,921	1900	64,387
1876	22,397	1901	77,920
1877	60,494	1902	38
1878	24,031	1903	2,515
1879	282,550	1904	71
1880	189,672	1905	682
1881	356,097	1906	106
1882	122,475	1907	20,217
1883	26,660	1908	23,061
1884	313,560	1909	24,173
1885	174,758	1910	24,225
1886	627	1911	24,119
1887	21,578	1912	24,796
1888	13,824	1913	45,707
1889	96,545	1914	45,351

Source: von Weiher, Überseegeschäft, appendix 11.

Table 10. Sales and Profits at Vienna I and II,
1878–1901/02

| Year | Sales | | Profits |
	Vienna I (M)	Vienna II (M)	(1,000 M)
1878			-12.2
1879	3,549		-1.0
1880	88,471		-29.3
1881	111,768		-20.1
1882	138,571		-24.1
1883	331,609		-12.3
1884	601,260		-62.3
1885	463,430		-74.7
1886	443,312		-81.6
1887	1,173,997		-20.9
1888	1,175,238	591,847	158.4
1889	2,408,379	2,367,390	61.4
1890	4,034,122	4,142,933	
1891	2,646,307	1,709,162	
1891/92	4,617,545	1,913,417	
1892/93	4,640,128	1,906,879	
1893/94	5,861,642	1,862,360	
1894/95	8,131,429	3,017,608	
1895/96	11,497,921	10,995,506	
1896/97	9,948,893	6,592,632	
1897/98	7,928,915	5,495,568	
1898/99	14,683,549	5,947,628	
1899/00		8,851,907	
1900/01		13,301,176	
1901/02		17,177,310	

Source: SAA 29/Li 435, 29/Li 935, and 20/Ld 366.
Note: Profits for the years 1878–80 are in 1,000 Austrian shillings.

Table 11. Net Profit Distributed to the Owners,
1850–1895/96 (in marks)

Year	Amount	Year	Amount
1850	12,375	1874	689,778
1851/52	26,035	1875	570,037
1853	33,750	1876	495,247
1854	43,205	1877	915,964
1855	142,988	1878	1,060,481
1856	57,177	1879	1,004,250
1857	57,905	1880	1,296,518
1858	97,860	1881	883,051
1859	65,531	1882	734,016
1860	60,456	1883	1,054,680
1861	10,752	1884	945,488
1862	3,049	1885	1,009,685
1863	26,067	1886	1,184,795
1864	75,015	1887	1,705,175
1865	119,857	1888	1,945,545
1866	164,002	1889	2,125,704
1867	122,632	1890	2,761,677
1868	260,661	1891	1,523,952
1869	349,695	1891/92	1,446,496
1870	438,303	1892/93	687,658
1871	549,213	1893/94	1,276,881
1872	446,148	1894/95	1,816,721
1873	726,540	1895/96	2,850,000

Source: SAA 14/Lh 662.

Table 12. Sales and Workforce, House of Siemens, 1871–1902/03

Year	Total Workforce	House of Siemens (not including foreign affiliates)	
		Workforce	Sales (1,000 marks)
1871	1,386	446	1760
1872	1,591	581	2,234
1873	1,672	628	3,381
1874	2,351	650	3,114
1875	1,119	571	2,700
1876	959	630	2,677
1877	1,329	738	3,712
1878	1,311	823	4,984
1879	2,128	754	5,023
1880	1,491	876	6,933
1881	2,453	905	4,962
1882	1,990	1,085	4,841
1883	2,326	1,300	5,583
1884	3,372	1,437	6,473
1885	2,751	1,568	6,769
1886	2,600	1,622	7,109
1887	3,025	2,078	9,511
1888	3,478	2,449	11,443
1889	4,513	3,084	16,782
1890	5,545	3,950	23,788
1891*	5,942	4,362	13,092
1891/92	6,533	4,775	19,661
1892/93	6,795	4,897	18,131
1893/94	7,833	5,389	23,605
1894/95	8,371	6,054	31,612
1895/96	10,340	7,697	53,498
1896/97	10,911	8,733	50,193
1897/98	11,445	9,058	57,217
1898/99	14,040	10,597	65,939
1899/00	16,350	12,283	76,809
1900/01	16,891	15,513	81,846
1901/02	17,823	14,659	76,552
1902/03	25,831	22,506	74,201

Source: SAA Z-report of May 26, 1966.
*Data only for January to July.

Appendix

Table 13. Sales and Workforce, House of Siemens
and DEG/AEG, 1884–1913

	Siemens		AEG
Year	Sales (million M)	Workforce	Sales (million M)
1884	6.5	1,437	1.2
1885	6.8	1,568	2.1
1886	7.1	1,622	2.2
1887	9.5	2,078	
1888	11.4	2,449	4.8
1889	16.7	3,084	6.2
1890	23.8	3,950	11.1
1891*	13.1	4,362	17.0
1892	19.7	4,775	13.1
1893	18.1	4,897	13.7
1894	23.6	5,389	16.3
1895	31.6	6,054	16.9
1896	53.5	7,697	39.2
1897	50.2	8,733	47.0
1898	57.3	9,058	64.0
1899	65.9	10,597	82.1
1900	76.8	12,283	100.2
1901	81.8	15,513	96.9
1902	76.6	14,659	80.6
1903	74.2	22,506	78.6
1904	89.6	24,246	108.3
1905	107.0	27,756	132.1
1906	135.6	30,644	175.5
1907	187.7	34,324	216.1
1908	211.5	33,162	237.2
1909	214.5	32,061	249.7
1910	228.8	38,457	252.0
1911	252.6	49,896	306.6
1912	329.7	58,497	379.2
1913	402.5	63,447	441.3

Source: SAA Z-report of May 26, 1966.
*Data only for January–July.

Table 14. Workforce and Sales, House of Siemens,
1903/04–1913/14

Year	Workforce, House of Siemens		Sales (million M)	
	Total	In Germany	S&H	SSW
1903/04	31,475	24,246	21.6	70.4
1904/05	35,258	27,756	26.2	84.0
1905/06	38,787	30,644	35.4	104.2
1906/07	42,866	34,324	49.4	144.3
1907/08	42,514	33,162	53.7	164.7
1908/09	41,303	32,061	60.1	160.5
1909/10	49,289	38,457	65.8	169.1
1910/11	64,016	49,896	64.2	195.4
1911/12	74,945	58,497	93.1	246.7
1912/13	81,795	63,447	97.0	318.3
1913/14	81,745	61,862	99.2	314.8

Source: SAA Z-report of May 26, 1966.

Notes

Introduction

1. In his studies of the "pure" theory of economy, Josef Alois Schumpeter (1883–1950) made an essential contribution to the analysis of the fluctuations of the state of the economy by pointing out the importance of innovations implemented by enterprises as impulses for the ups and downs of the economy (*Business Cycles*). (In the notes, titles of publications are given in abbreviated form. For more detailed references, see the bibliography at the end of the book.)

2. The term *electrical industry* is defined as follows: (*a*) Technologically, the electrical industry is characterized by goods and services for the generation, production, transformation, distribution, and application of electrical energy. (*b*) Business units of enterprises are considered part of the electrical industry if the predominant part of their activities involves the goods and services listed under (*a*). See Sawall, "Unternehmenskonzentration," p. 11.

3. In his memoirs Werner von Siemens equates the founding of the Electrotechnical Society in Germany in 1879 with the identification of the initial activities of electrical engineering as a special branch of technology. The term *electrotechnical,* describing technical applications of the science of electricity, was used for the first time in German in the name of that association. Werner von Siemens, *Lebenserinnerungen* (Memoirs), p. 280.

4. Ten years earlier Faraday had laid the foundations for the development of electric motors with the construction of his "rotary device." Volta called the galvanic element an electromotor. This term was widely used for years and explains the term *electromotive force.* See Dettmar, *Entwicklung,* p. 12.

5. Shortly after Michael Faraday had established the law of induction, the Frenchman Antoine Hippolyte Pixii built a small genera-

tor for electricity using a simple horseshoe-shaped magnet made of steel revolving around a horseshoe-shaped electromagnet. Even though this first machine was of no particular practical use, it initiated a series of experiments with electromagnetic machines, instruments, and motors.

6. Manufacturing in preindustrial times was characterized by an intracompany system of production and by the predominant use of manual work. At the time Siemens went into business, factories had already combined production in large work units, unlike the so-called cottage industry; however, in contrast to the factories that were established later, such work units were not yet mechanized. Until 1867, when electric power engineering started to fundamentally revolutionize the structure of production, the Telegraph System Construction Enterprise Siemens & Halske differed from the traditional manual trade shop as well as from those who contracted out and from cottage industry in the following respects: by its use of capital accounting; by the formally free and contractually regulated character of the manual work performed in its facilities; by its separation of the workplace from the workers' residences; by its size; and by the increasing centralization of the work processes. On the other hand, the company could not be called a fully developed factory, since the dominant form of production was still the cooperation of adjacent shops producing the same or similar devices. Like specialization in the manufacturing of specific products—a practice that gradually took hold as new branches of production were opened up—specialization with respect to the steps of production grew very slowly. In contrast to the majority of engineering shops in Prussia, until 1870 the machinery at Siemens & Halske consisted almost exclusively of nonspecialized machines. In 1863, for the first time, a steam engine was installed. See Kocka, *Angestellten,* pp. 24ff.

7. In 1888 hereditary nobility was bestowed on Werner Siemens. For purposes of uniformity, he is called Werner von Siemens throughout this book.

8. See Ehrenberg, *Unternehmungen;* Matschoß, *Werner Siemens;* Weiher, *Werner von Siemens.*

9. Kocka, "Siemens," p. 131.

10. Although Werner von Siemens, because of his knowledge and his distinguished position in the government Telegraph Commission, had good prospects of becoming the director of the Prussian State Telegraph Service, he preferred to be an independent businessman, as

he stated in a letter to his brother Wilhelm, dated January 3, 1847: " . . . the tempting prospect, to rise to the position of director of the future Prussian Telegraph Service due to my outstanding role in the Telegraph Commission. I turned this offer down, since employment in civil service is not to my taste and I am convinced that I can do more for the world and myself if I secure absolute independence for myself" (Siemens Archives Files [SAA] WP Briefe [Letters]).

11. See Werner von Siemens, *Lebenserinnerungen,* p. 29. From the outset, Werner von Siemens expressly stipulated that the firm should concentrate primarily on manufacturing, not on activities as a contractor. He mentioned the reasons that led him to adopt this business principle in a letter to his brother Wilhelm, November 11, 1876: "Supplying goods forms a sure ground for continuing business, whereas contractor work is only profitable if the conditions are particularly favorable. An exclusive engagement as a contractor . . . flourishes only temporarily. A company engaged in producing and selling goods may outlast many generations, and that is more to my taste" (SAA WP Briefe).

12. See scientific and technical studies by Werner von Siemens, vol. 1, *Abhandlungen,* pp. 208–10.

13. SAA WP Briefe.

14. Hertner, "Enterprises," p. 91.

15. The perspectives that were behind such a management strategy are evident in a letter written by Werner von Siemens on May 13, 1863, to his brother Wilhelm: "As we are not able to perform foreign and distant investments profitably from here (Berlin), we had to establish firms in Russia, England, and Vienna, which can do business and make profitable use of our activities here with the help of our advance in telegraphy, supported by our manufacturing and capital as well as by our personal engagement here in Berlin, if necessary" (SAA WP Briefe).

16. Werner von Siemens clearly stated his objections in writing his memoirs in a letter to his daughter Anna, July 22, 1892: "For me the most important aspect is less the stylistic correctness of my notes, but that the plain truth about my feelings and thinking is reflected. I must be able to recognize myself in all parts, otherwise the whole thing will appear alien to me. Besides, I consider it to be a typical German mistake that our way of writing differs from our way of speaking. People should clearly recognize the individuality behind both one's writing and speaking" (SAA WP Briefe).

17. SAA WP Briefe.

18. The analyses by Kocka and Conrad on internal business structures are particularly good. Extensive studies on enterprises abroad before 1880 are few, however. Important information is given in the master's thesis by Jost Schmidt, Bonn, Germany, to which I had access by courtesy of the author. Apart from these, one must fall back on older literature, which does not always satisfy stringent academic criteria.

19. For this assessment see, above all, Kocka, *Unternehmensverwaltung,* p. 53. See also Werner's letter to Wilhelm, July 7, 1866: "If the Germans should succeed in rising to the high level of the present situation and support the formation of a unified and strong Germany with Prussia at the top, instead of crying for their expelled princes or those trembling with fear anticipating such a fate, our children will obtain a real Fatherland and bless Bismarck and the Prussian Army." A similar overtone can be detected in a letter to Wilhelm, September 25, 1866: "I am deeply convinced now that Bismarck is moved by the sacred spirit of a grand national mission, that he is resolved not to create a half-baked Germany but a whole and integral nation. This is the reason why I have detached myself from most of my former political friends and have campaigned and voted for the vote of confidence in his foreign policy" (SAA WP Briefe).

Chapter 1

1. See Loewe, "Industrie," p. 119; Kocka, "Siemens," p. 125.

2. The first stage of development of the telegraph industry in particular was characterized by enterprises that, in addition to their customary activities, adjusted to the requirements of governmental or private telegraphy. These primarily handwork-oriented firms, in the course of registration of "commercial conditions," were first classified as part of the category "Mechanical artisans and craftsmen" within the subgroup "Mechanics for mathematical, optical, physical and surgical instruments." Wessel, *Entwicklung,* pp. 141ff.

3. For 1890 a detailed list of production exists, published by the Central Association of the Electrical Industry (in million marks):

Electric motors and generators	5.5
Transformers	0.5
Storage batteries and other batteries	4.5
Switchgear and equipment	0.3
Equipment and tools for installation	0.3
Cables and insulated wires	8.0
Electric tools	0.1
Household appliances	0.2
Chandeliers	0.2
Lamps	0.3
Equipment and devices for communication via cables and overhead lines	3.6
Equipment for timing, signaling, and safety instrumentation	0.2
Active and passive components	0.2
Measuring, testing, and controlling instruments	0.3
Electromedical instruments and equipment	0.3
Electrographite	1.5
Repair services	3.9

See *Dynamik.*

4. Peschke, *Elektroindustrie*, p. 100.

5. Borchardt, *Revolution*, p. 187.

6. In Germany in 1850, a total of 85.9 million letters and post-cards and 40,000 telegrams were mailed. By 1873 the volume of mail had increased to 563 million letters and 10.8 million telegrams. Kocka, *Unternehmensverwaltung*, p. 45.

7. Johann Philipp Reis (1834–74) constructed the first operational electric telephone, which he demonstrated as the "wooden ear" to an assembly of the Association of Physicists in Frankfurt on October 26, 1861. The device exhibited by Reis was at that time considered to be only an interesting gadget for demonstration and soon fell into oblivion. About fifteen years later Alexander Graham Bell and Elisha Gray in the United States filed applications for patents for electromagnetic telephones. By the invention and refinement of the carbon microphone, Edison, Emile Berliner, and David Hughes in the United States and Blake in England made essential contributions to the improvement of the telephone service. On January 28, 1878, the first public telephone exchange in the world was opened in the United States in New Haven, Connecticut. The first telephone office in Ger-

many was opened on January 12, 1881, in Berlin. For data on the development of the telephone sector, see also the tables in the appendix.

8. Between 1885 and 1900 telephone charges dropped from 1 mark to 20 pfennigs per unit; the flat rate for the direct exchange lines was lowered with networks—which had up to fifty direct exchange lines—from 200 marks annually to 80 marks. Tilly, "Verkehrswesen," p. 579.

9. The blight of the potato disease in 1845–46 and grain crop failures in 1846 and 1847 had led to famines in almost all parts of Germany. The excessive demand on the population's purchasing power led to a failure in the demand for material goods, a development that affected the craft sector most severely; yet the investment goods industry, which had witnessed an impressive uptrend since the beginning of the 1840s, was also affected by slumps at the peak of the crisis. The policy of promoting the craft sector, which Prussia had vigorously pursued until 1844, was replaced by restrictive measures. Borchardt, *Revolution,* pp. 153, 159–60.

10. As a result of the so-called *Gründerkrise,* the Reichstag passed a customs tariff marking the end of the German free–trade policy and constituting the beginning of a tariff policy against foreign countries; restrictiveness thereafter tended to increase until the start of World War I. The tariffs began as a response to economic difficulties faced by the overexpanded heavy industry and the cotton-processing industry of southern Germany. Also, agriculture east of the Elbe River (in eastern Germany) began to suffer from competition for cheaper foreign foodstuffs.

11. Wagenführ, *Bedeutung,* pp. 36ff.

12. Feldenkirchen, "Export," p. 307.

13. In Germany this was true, for example, for the potash industry before 1914 and also for the dyestuff industry.

14. Borchardt, "Wachstum," p. 235.

Chapter 2

1. Werner von Siemens, *Lebenserinnerungen,* pp. 13, 16.

2. There was no feasible relief from tariff duties, as there was in England and France, because Germany until the 1870s was a grain-exporting country that could not risk retaliation on its own farm products.

3. Werner von Siemens, *Lebenserinnerungen,* p. 9.

4. Werner to Carl, Charlottenburg, December 25, 1887, SAA WP Briefe.

5. Kocka, *Unternehmer,* p. 52; also pp. 30–34.

6. See, for example, the statement Johann Georg Siemens made about his son, then chief executive officer of the Deutsche Bank, as late as 1870: "My son, the clerk." Helfferich, *Georg von Siemens,* vol. 3, pp. 153, 159.

7. Wilhelm to Werner, London, February 11, 1844, SAA WP Briefe.

8. SAA 2/Lr 68.

9. Werner von Siemens, *Lebenserinnerungen,* p. 13.

10. Wilhelm to Werner, Manchester, July 1, 1847, SAA WP Briefe.

11. Werner to Wilhelm, Berlin, March 11, 1848, SAA WP Briefe.

12. Werner to Wilhelm, Berlin, March 20, 1848, SAA WP Briefe.

Chapter 3

1. Pohl, *Aufbruch,* pp. 238ff.

2. In the autumn of 1846 Werner Siemens had just begun analyzing the insulating qualities of gutta-percha, which had only recently been discovered. Jacketing a copper wire with gutta-percha met with difficulties at first. The problem was solved by the gutta-percha press, which was developed by Werner Siemens and Johann Georg Halske and consisted of a cylinder filled with heated gutta-percha, through which the wire was run while pressure was applied to the cylinder. Trendelenburg, *Geschichte,* p. 3.

3. On the organization of the state telegraph network, see *Elektronische Zeitschrift,* p. 31. The organization of the state telegraph network was begun in the following states and years:

Great Britain	1845	The Netherlands	1852
Switzerland	1852	Germany	1849
Sweden	1853	Austria	1849
Norway	1855	Belgium	1849
Spain	1855	Portugal	1855

4. Kocka, *Unternehmensverwaltung,* p. 63.

5. Georg Siemens, *Weg,* vol. 1, p. 23.

6. Werner von Siemens, publicly describing the causes for the defects, recommended learning from the mistakes; yet he advised against changing hastily to the construction and use of overhead lines, since with the invention of the seamless lead shield for cables he had succeeded in greatly improving the outer insulation of the cables. Since the authorities feared his argument was biased, Werner von Siemens proposed "a careful comparative analysis of the results collected so far by scientific and competent experts." Nottebohm in particular took this suggestion as a personal affront and canceled all state orders awarded to S & H.

7. Pole, *Wilhelm Siemens,* p. 105.

8. In the 1860s the production of water meters proceeded favorably and the resulting profits were considerable. SAA 29/Lp 586.

9. Kocka, *Unternehmensverwaltung,* p. 67.

10. Werner to Wilhelm, Paris, April 26, 1850, SAA WP Briefe.

11. The opening of a Siemens branch under the name of Siemens Frères in France in 1878 was a consequence of French patent legislation. According to this legislation, inventions for which patents were issued in France had to be produced there, within a certain time limit, if the claim for the patent was to be maintained. In 1886 this branch was closed, however, as the demand from French industry had not been as great as hoped. The losses of this branch were put at 1.3 million francs. Siemens later tried to open up the French market via cooperation with domestic firms. SAA 68/Li 177.

12. Quoted from Weiher, *Carl von Siemens,* p. 17.

13. Werner to Carl, Berlin, December 16, 1852, SAA WP Briefe.

14. Werner von Siemens, *Lebenserinnerungen,* p. 125.

15. Friedrichsort, July 25, 1848, SAA WP Briefe.

16. Werner to Carl, Berlin, June 26, 1854, SAA WP Briefe.

17. SAA 21/Li 53, Gesellschaftsverträge.

18. These numbers are a very cautious estimate taken from Kirchner, *Deutsche Industrie,* pp. 47ff.; for different figures see Weiher, *Carl von Siemens,* p. 16.

19. Werner von Siemens, *Lebenserinnerungen,* p. 150.

20. Ehrenberg, *Unternehmungen,* pp. 103–5.

21. Carl to Werner, February 17, 1864, SAA WP Briefe.

22. Werner to Carl, April 2, 1881, SAA WP Briefe.

23. SAA 20/Ld 366, 2, p. 53.

24. Carl to Werner, February 16 and 28, 1881, SAA WP Briefe.

25. Werner to Carl, February 6, 1882, SAA WP Briefe.

26. Carl to Werner, March 30, 1882, SAA WP Briefe.

27. Werner to Carl, March 21, 1887, SAA WP Briefe.

28. Kocka, *Unternehmensverwaltung*, p. 78.

29. Weiher, *Überseegeschäft*, pp. 38–39; Kieve, *Telegraph*, pp. 77ff.

30. See "Beiträge zur Theorie der Legung und Untersuchung submariner Telegraphenleitungen," 1874; see also Werner von Siemens, *Lebenserinnerungen*, pp. 151–56.

31. For purposes of uniformity, Wilhelm—William—Siemens is called by the name Wilhelm throughout.

32. Wilhelm to Werner, London, February 21, 1862, SAA WP Briefe.

33. For Werner's personal assessment of this misfortune, see Werner von Siemens, *Lebenserinnerungen*, p. 179.

34. See Werner's complaints in his letters to Carl, e.g., May 20, 1863, and August 31, 1863, SAA WP Briefe.

35. Werner to Wilhelm, Berlin, May 7, 1864, SAA WP Briefe.

36. Pole, *Wilhelm Siemens*, pp. 140–49.

37. Ehrenberg, *Unternehmungen*, pp. 270–71.

38. SAA 21/Li 53. Also see table 11 in the appendix, showing the surplus net profit distributed to the owners.

39. Werner to Carl, March 4, 1867, SAA WP Briefe.

40. See the letter from Werner to Wilhelm, January 18, 1859: "Already in this year we will make more profit because (as will be proved soon) of the piece-rate work which we have now introduced, and profits will surely increase as piece rates are used more and as we get more work" (SAA WP Briefe).

Chapter 4

1. Kocka, *Unternehmensverwaltung*, p. 117.

2. See Peschke, *Elektroindustrie*, pp. 48–56.

3. In 1831 Faraday demonstrated induction: if a conductor, e.g., a wire (or a wire wound into a coil), is moved through a magnetic field, a voltage will be generated in that conductor. Soon afterward the first electromagnetic machines were constructed, in which an armature (rotor) carrying coils rotated in the field of a permanent

magnet. Owing to the low intensity of the field of such a magnet (stator), only low electrical power was generated. Sometimes electromagnets with cores made of magnetically soft iron and fitted with coils energized by current drawn from external batteries were used, in place of permanent magnets, in the stator.

Werner von Siemens discovered that some magnetism (residual magnetism) remained in the iron cores if some direct current had passed, even for only an instant, through a coil enclosing the core. If an armature was rotated in the low residual field of a stator, a low voltage was induced in the armature. If a closed loop was set up and the initially low current driven by the low voltage was routed through the coils of the stator, the magnetic field of the stator was reinforced, and a correspondingly larger voltage was induced in the rotating armature. By this process of self-excitation, magnetism in the rotor and stator quickly increased until the iron cores were almost completely magnetically saturated. No longer were external batteries required for excitation of the magnets.

In his experiments Werner von Siemens made use of his experiences with a type of armature he had developed in 1856 during attempts to replace the expensive batteries necessary for operating long-distance telegraph lines. The iron core of this generator had a cross section of iron resembling two opposed capital letter Ts.

Although the pilot type of the "dynamomachine" built by Werner von Siemens had a maximum rating of only 50 watts and accordingly was just an experimental device, successive improvements to this machine created, within a few years, the basis for the tremendous growth of electrical power technology. The new technology permitted the efficient and convenient conversion of large amounts of mechanical energy into electrical energy, the distribution of electrical energy, and the simple reconversion of electrical into mechanical energy in factories and households.

At the end of 1875, the design of the slotted cylindrical armature with distributed windings and a commutator consisting of many prismatic segments, invented by Friedrich von Hefner-Alteneck, had reached a level of advancement allowing Siemens & Halske to offer a series of standardized generators with ratings of up to 5 kilowatts. A catalog describing these generators and quoting prices was published. In 1877 Siemens sold 91 of these machines; in the following year, 271; and in 1879, 351. While the quantity of machines produced remained more or less constant, their ratings increased almost exponentially in subsequent years. At the turn of the century, generators rating 1,000 kilowatts were sold.

4. See also table 4 in the appendix, showing the turnover in the time period 1847–96, divided by product groups.

5. Carl Frischen soon developed for Siemens & Halske a new signal system for railways, which achieved international acceptance. Later he was promoted to the position of director of manufacturing facilities.

6. "Oddly, Werner Siemens did not expect these people to become useful coworkers. Most likely in the later periods of his life he was unable to detach himself from the notion of one head alone, his own, as being sufficient for the scientific analysis of emerging problems. This concept had doubtlessly been mostly correct for his first two decades at the helm of his firm. Perhaps he also shared the mistrust of many self–made men against people who might make great demands right from the beginning of their employment, because of their educational background, that they would be entitled to only later and based on achievement" (Georg Siemens, *Weg*, vol. 1, p. 71).

7. For the growth in the number of employees, see tables 12–14 in the appendix.

8. For more details on the relationship between Berlin and London, see Weiher, *Überseegeschäft*.

9. Pole, *Wilhelm Siemens*, pp. 177ff.; Georg Siemens, *Weg*, vol. 1, pp. 58ff.

10. Werner to Wilhelm, Berlin, August 14, 1867, SAA WP Briefe.

11. Werner to Carl, April 5, 1867, and Werner to Wilhelm, May 12, 1867, in Matschoß, *Werner Siemens*, vol. 1, pp. 26ff., 270ff.

12. Georg Siemens, *Weg*, vol. 1, p. 64.

13. Werner to Carl, Berlin, January 24, 1867, SAA WP Briefe.

14. Since the original documents were destroyed, the figures are quoted according to Ehrenberg, *Unternehmungen*, p. 264.

15. February 10, 1870, in Matschoß, *Werner Siemens*, vol. 2, p. 318.

16. Werner von Siemens gave a detailed description of his feelings in his memoirs, pp. 279ff.

17. Quoted by Weiher, *Carl von Siemens*, p. 105.

18. On the financial development of Siemens Brothers, see table 9 in the appendix.

19. Quoted in Heintzenberg, "Carl Heinrich von Siemens," p. 111.

20. For detailed explanation of the technical particulars, see Georg Siemens, *Weg*, vol. 1, pp. 89–107.

21. Werner to Wilhelm, Berlin, December 5, 1878, in Matschoß, *Werner Siemens*, vol. 2, p. 582: "If there is no more to Edison's invention, it is not worth much."

22. Werner wrote to his brother Wilhelm on March 8, 1883: "In reality the German Edison Company will therefore be an installation agency for installing the machines, and the other materials (for transmission of electric power, etc.) we produce" (Matschoß, *Werner Siemens,* vol. 2, p. 771).

23. As Wilhelm von Siemens wrote, "The concept of growth in a greenhouse is alien to the spirit forming the base of the entire Siemens enterprise. This approach is easy to understand if the following fact is taken into consideration: The principal holder of shares of S & H, the Siemens family, which has the greatest influence on the management, cannot be interested in raising the capital of the company by offering more shares to the public. In fact, a conservative and merely manufacturers' policy has been pursued" (SAA 4/Ld 147). Elsewhere Wilhelm von Siemens expressed the differences in the business policy of AEG and Siemens: "In all the life and activities of Rathenau I cannot find any outstanding achievement by Rathenau as an engineer that could be classified as being worthy of an engineer, i.e., any accomplishment making him appear to be an inventor or innovative designer opening new and previously unknown vistas. What he has achieved in the field of technology is merely the transplantation of American designs and methods of production into German soil, and their natural development" (SAA 11/Lb 569).

24. By means of a contract dated March 13, 1883, DEG obtained from Edison and his legal assigns the exclusive right for the use of Edison's inventions within the territorial limits of the German Reich. Emil Rathenau planned to introduce incandescent lighting, the importance of which had not been fully recognized by Werner von Siemens, systematically in Berlin and throughout Germany.

Siemens & Halske acquired licenses on the Edison patents marketed by AEG, while DEG pledged in a contract to leave the manufacturing of generators, motors, cables, and instrumentation to Siemens & Halske. Siemens & Halske gave up the right to build central power stations to DEG. Owing to the terms of this contract, Siemens & Halske developed into a more and more specialized firm, providing equipment and accessories for central power stations. However, by 1887, shortly after it had been signed, both parties felt the contract to be obstructive to their business activities and agreed upon a revision. In 1894 all contractual commitments were annulled. For the correspondence on this matter, with a detailed analysis of the reasons, see SAA 29/Li 435, 46/Lh 287; AEG Archives, minutes of the committee of the advisory board; Archive Deutsche Bank catalogue AEG S 76 and 79; "Fünfzig Jahre AEG," pp. 39ff.

25. For the beginnings of the Schuckert enterprise, see Keuth, *Schuckert*.

26. During the first stage of the enterprise, the technically oriented Sigmund Schuckert had concentrated on production. With the full entry of Alexander Wacker into the management of the firm, emphasis shifted onto financial affairs and onto the contracting business. Wacker had initially been Schuckert's general representative for the central and northern parts of Germany. See SAA 28/Li 987; Cohen, *Schuckert*, pp. 39ff.

27. Initially, owing to the small amount of initial capital required, ordinary partnership (*offene Handelsgesellschaft—OHG*) was the preferred legal structure of electrotechnical enterprises. At the end of the 1880s, many firms were converted into limited partnerships (*Kommanditgesellschaft—KG*). With the rapid growth of the electrical industry in the 1890s, numerous enterprises went public (*Aktiengesellschaft—AG*). Three corporations—AEG, Union-Elektrizitäts–Gesellschaft, and Helios—were founded directly as public companies. Fasolt, "Elektrizitätsgesellschaften," pp. 3ff.

28. In 1894 several banks founded the Association for Electrical Projects (Gesellschaft für Elektrische Unternehmungen) in order to finance the projects of the Union firm. Within a few years all large electrical companies had established at least one similar financing company. Feldenkirchen, "Finanzierung," p. 103.

29. See also the remarks in the memoirs of Felix Deutsch, the subsequent chief executive officer of AEG:

Particularly the newer of these firms had the idea of the "contractor business" of AEG as being very simple and obviously very lucrative, and engaged themselves intensively in this field. Whereas we, however, set about with great care and reserve, the rival firms, although—or, because—they did not by far have the same amount of resources and experience in the fields of technology, economics, and organization at their disposal as we had, plunged carelessly and wildly into all licenses and authorized exorbitant fees to be paid to the cities and impossible conditions for the transfer of the plants to the municipal authorities. In addition, in our contracts with our affiliated firms we used to set the profit for the items we supplied at a very low rate, since we always had the profitability of the projects in mind, as from the very beginning it was clear to us that we could not continually reduce our liquidity by financing large central power stations with our own capital. Rather we tried to follow the concept of establishing such stations using our own resources, but as soon as possible leaving them to independent companies, in order to keep our capital liquid for new business activities. Consequently, we had to be careful to establish only sound and viable enterprises, whereas the competitors, contrary to our concept, saw their main business in charging their affiliated firms high prices, thus providing large earnings to the parent firm, without any concern for the economical operation and profitability of the power plants. (From documents in the Leo Baeck Institute, New York)

30. The first enterprises, such as the Berlin Electric Power Plants, concentrated chiefly on supplying electrical energy for illumination and only secondarily supplied firms with electrical energy for mechanical power. After the power plants were first put into operation, ten years passed before a noticeable increase in power consumption for mechanical purposes was registered. By about the end of the nineteenth century, the usage of electricity for operational purposes had become the dominant reason for the construction of new central electrical power plants. As most of the power stations were erected by the industrial enterprises themselves, the share of the public power stations in the total production of electrical energy dropped from 44.4% in 1891 to 19.5% in 1900.

31. Sawall, "Unternehmenskonzentration," p. 68.

32. In 1890 after the death of Carl Frischen, who had headed the railway department of Siemens & Halske, to meet the increasing demand the firm founded a separate central office for electric railways. Frischen, who had previously been director of the telegraph system of

the railways of the kingdom of Hanover in northern Germany, had in 1870 invented the track sectioning safety system for railways, a fundamental invention, which served as the basis for comprehensive railway safety systems later developed by Siemens & Halske. Such systems prevent collisions by keeping an oncoming train from entering a section of track on which there is already another train.

33. Years that horse-drawn and electric streetcar lines were started in German cities:

City	Horse-drawn streetcars	Electric streetcars
Berlin	1865	1879, 1896
Hamburg	1866	1893
Stuttgart	1868	1895
Leipzig	1872	1896
Frankfurt	1872	1884, 1899
Dresden	1872	1893
Hanover	1872	1893
Danzig	1873	1896
Wiesbaden	1875	1896
Düsseldorf	1876	1896
Elberfeld	1876	1896
Barmen	1876	1894
Munich	1876	1895
Karlsruhe	1877	1898
Cologne	1877	1901
Breslau	1877	1893
Kassel	1877	1898
Magdeburg	1877	1899
Mannheim	1878	1900
Aachen	1880	1895
Halle	1882	1891

34. See also Wilhelm von Siemens's entry in his diary, December 26, 1902:

> We, that is S & H, have often been reproached for having allowed AEG, Schuckert, Union, Lahmeyer, Brown Boveri to grow that large. But AEG became so large through their concession in Berlin, through which they earned some 50 million, and through the Deutsche Bank. They (AEG) were deliberately introduced to both opportunities by Werner Siemens under the slogan: S & H shall be the manufacturers and inventors, AEG the constructors. . . . S & H would have required hundreds of millions to control the situation. We have also stuck to our family policy and wanted to stay masters in our home. . . . During this period of time S & H has maintained a high level technically, and has in reality risen considerably when compared with the past era's Frischen-Hefner. At present the technical reputation of S & H is at its peak. Besides, the enterprise rests on a secure and safe base. The financial affairs are in good shape, the cash deposits at the banks exceed 10 million. . . . The year 1903 will probably decide the question whether Rathenau intends to make additional sections of the industry financially dependent on him or whether S & H will come to some agreement with Schuckert in order to represent a greater counterbalance. The matter is being considered right now.

35. Union was founded by the Loewe, Thyssen, and Thomson-Houston International Electric Company. The firm Ludwig Loewe took over manufacturing. In 1897, 50% of all track and electrically powered streetcars of the electric railways in Europe were constructed according to the Thomson–Houston system. In 1898 Union purchased the electric factories from Ludwig Loewe. Union constructed streetcar systems in Erfurt, Leipzig, Barmen, Elberfeld, Elbing, Solingen, Düsseldorf, Duisburg, Berlin, Meissen, and Magdeburg (SAA 29/Ls 336). Since the 1880s, firms such as Aron, Mix & Genest, Voigt & Haeffner—to name only a few active in the fields of electrical power technology as well as electrical signaling and communications technology—had been established, occupying special niches within the overall production. See Czada, *Elektroindustrie*, p. 43.

36. Pohl, *Geschichte*, p. 158.

37. SAA 68/Lb 947.

38. See Werner von Siemens's letter to Eugen von der Weyde, October 25, 1884, SAA 68/Lb 947, where further examples of rejections can be found.

39. SAA 16/La 92.

40. See contract with Rau to serve as a representative, June 21, 1882, SAA 68/Li 312.

41. SAA 68/Li 312.

42. Werner von Siemens to Carlo Moleschott, December 31, 1890, SAA 32/Lh 678.

43. Eibert, *Unternehmenspolitik*, pp. 206ff., 216–21; Pohl, *Rathenau*, pp. 53, 140–64; Chandler, *Scale and Scope*, p. 216.

44. In the 105th meeting of the third study group of subcommittee no. 3 for commerce, on May 14, 1929, the director general of Siemens & Halske, Dr. Adolf Franke, was asked by the experts, among other subjects, about the sales abroad and the marketing organization. Franke informed them that sales at home were organized by the Technical Offices, whereas sales abroad were organized by the firm's own companies.

> We created the system of the firm's own companies, which in most places has resulted in a financially sound situation. We can keep a tighter rein on them, guide them in certain directions, and make their prices mandatory. They can be handled in a way impossible with an independent agent. This is the reason why we have extended this system all over the world, with the exception of a few countries, mainly in cooperation with Siemens-Schuckert [an enterprise formed after Werner's death]. . . . They submit useful suggestions, and we receive more information about the activities of our competitors. We get better reports than from the agents, and thus new ideas. . . . We experienced much better progress with companies of our own than with agents. This includes a lot of plants constructed and put into service by our own installation offices. There is also a lot of repair work taken care of immediately, on the spot, and in this respect as well, companies of our own are more useful for us than independent agents. (SAA 11/Lg 724, Franke's official papers)

45. SAA 47/Lg 742.

46. The workshops established before 1863 in London and St. Petersburg took care of the maintenance and installation of products manufactured in Berlin.

47. Waller, *Studien,* vol. 3, pp. 100–103.
48. SAA 23/Lk 677.
49. See tables 4 and 6 in the appendix showing S & H's sales in different regions.
50. See Werner von Siemens, *Lebenserinnerungen,* p. 241: "I can only strongly advise proceeding in the same way in our colonial efforts. Simple people with extremely modest needs are averse to all cultural developments. Only after a desire for more elevated needs has been aroused and they have become used to work as a means to satisfy those needs will such people become receptive to social and religious and cultural endeavors. To start with the latter will merely produce illusory results."
51. Wilhelm to Werner, June 28, 1868: "It would be preferable to set up the mutual agreements in such a fashion as to make the future course of our activities less dependent on the personal existence [of the participants], and when we meet next time we must endeavor to find such a solution! It would be unwise to reduce our activities, but it is more and more imperative to concentrate our energy on essential affairs, as has been shown by these losses but also by our awareness of our own deficiencies" (SAA WP Briefe).
52. Werner to Carl, Ragaz, July 17–18, 1868, SAA WP Briefe.
53. Heintzenberg, *Carl Siemens,* p. 128.

Chapter 5

1. See Werner's letter to his son Wilhelm, February 3, 1877: "In my younger days it was particularly depressing for me to see so much poverty and misery at home and yet to be unable to help alleviate these conditions and to have little prospect of being capable of doing so in later years. Admittedly, these circumstances were also a great spur for me to work hard" (SAA WP Briefe).
2. Charlottenburg, December 25, 1887, SAA WP Briefe.
3. Carl to Werner, St. Petersburg, December 21, 1887, SAA WP Briefe.
4. Heintzenberg, *Carl Siemens,* p. 87.
5. For more detailed information on these problems, see Weiher, *Überseegeschäft,* pp. 131–37.
6. December 25, 1884, in Matschoß, *Werner Siemens,* vol. 2, p. 837.
7. Quoted by Weiher, *Überseegeschäft,* p. 163.

8. Carl to Werner, St. Petersburg, December 21, 1887: "Why should we accept strangers as replacements for people who have passed away? After my death, according to my last will, my son will replace me and you will probably do the same with your sons. What strangers mean, we have seen with Löffler and Louis S." (SAA WP Briefe).

9. Werner to Carl, Charlottenburg, December 25, 1887, SAA WP Briefe.

10. Kocka, "Siemens."

11. Limited partnership agreement, St. Petersburg, December 27, 1889; Berlin, January 10, 1890, paragraph 13, SAA 21/Li 53.

12. See letter from Werner to Carl, November 22, 1854: "There is a shortage of mechanics. . . . It is difficult to find reliable workers" (SAA WP Briefe)

13. June 16, 1868, in Matschoß, *Werner Siemens,* vol. 1, p. 292.

14. Within the personnel of the Telegraph System Construction Enterprise, members of the following groups rated as key officials: persons holding the power of attorney, accountants, heads of workshops, cashiers, file clerks, workshop masters, workshop writers, persons in charge of materials, designers, and office staff.

15. Until 1872 the enterprise had not adopted any internal administrative regulations or guidelines at all. Starting in 1860, the first person holding the power of attorney, senior engineer William Meyer, who had increasingly taken over the internal management of the enterprise, received 5% of the profit from the total business as a reward. Carl Haase, the accountant who structured the bookkeeping of the firm into a system that remained in use well into the twentieth century, received 2.5% of the profits from the Berlin business, as did the head of the workshop, Weiss.

16. Ragaz, July 17–18, 1868, SAA WP Briefe.

17. Werner to Carl, July 18, 1868, SAA WP Briefe.

18. Conrad, *Erfolgsbeteiligung,* p. 120; Czada, *Elektroindustrie,* p. 119.

19. Werner von Siemens, *Lebenserinnerungen,* p. 283.

20. For this reason, Werner von Siemens regarded the firm's insurance programs also as an apt means to fight against the "strike mania" (*Streikmanie*). See Werner von Siemens, *Lebenserinnerungen,* p. 201.

21. Werner von Siemens, *Lebenserinnerungen,* p. 202.

22. SAA WP Briefe.

23. Werner von Siemens, *Lebenserinnerungen,* p. 207.

24. Werner von Siemens, *Lebenserinnerungen,* p. 209.

Chapter 6

1. As well as the Deutsche Bank, the Mitteldeutsche Credit–Bank acted for Siemens & Halske between 1890 and 1929, when the merger with the Commerz- und Privatbank took place. This bank also participated in the founding of electrical enterprises in Germany, Switzerland, Russia, and Brazil. Other banks became important to a greater extent for Siemens in the 1920s. See SAA 11/Lh 504; BA Potsdam, Ba 2, Deutsche Bank No. 18855.

2. Weiher and Goetzeler, *Weg,* p. 44.

3. Archive of the Deutsche Bank, Siemens file, p. 1347.

4. For this reason, Georg Siemens resigned from his post as a member of the supervisory board of AEG. Archive of the Deutsche Bank, Siemens Cash Assets, p. 1348.

5. Note also the opinion expressed by Georg Siemens of the Deutsche Bank on the business rules of Siemens & Halske AG: "I have never seen such a brake as this instruction. The theory of the law requires the supervisory board to supervise, or to know everything; the theory of the draft of the business rules of Siemens & Halske requires the supervisory board to possess the [sole] authority to approve everything, without it nothing may be done. By these means all jurisdiction of the top management is wiped out. As the representative of the Deutsche Bank I would advise against long-term agreements with an institution managed in such a fashion." The following definition in the rules was responsible for such an attitude:

> In order to achieve uniform handling of the business operations in the individual divisions and a purposeful cooperation between the divisions involved in an individual case, the supervisory board will appoint a delegate. He will be vested with the right to order a different allocation of the business operations and particularly to appoint, in addition to the responsible supervisors installed according to the business rules, additional supervisors on special occasions. This delegate, by executing the right the supervisory board and its chairman are entitled to, will moreover be authorized to supervise the entire conduct of business of the board of management and also to issue instructions to the board of management. With respect to decisions on fundamental problems, the department heads will get in touch with this delegate in time. This applies particularly to matters affecting the spheres of several divisions. (SAA 33/Ld 603)

The first board of management was composed exclusively of members of the Siemens family. In the spring of 1898, A. von Gwinner from the Deutsche Bank was elected to the board, and later Carl Klönne, on April 19, 1900. After Roland Lücke joined the board in January 1901, Gwinner resigned on January 4, 1902, since Deutsche Bank disapproved of three directors of the bank being members of the supervisory board of a single company at the same time. BA Potsdam, Assets 80, Ba 2, Deutsche Bank No. 18850.

6. SAA 33/Ld 603.

7. Georg Siemens, *Weg,* vol. 1, p. 188.

8. Georg Siemens, *Weg,* vol. 1, pp. 132ff. Also compare paragraph 25 quoted above with the following comment by Wilhelm von Siemens: "The organization of our company indeed exhibits an abnormality due to the historical and financial position of the Siemens family in the company. We formed a corporation in 1897 but kept all our shares and have taken out new ones. We did not intend to give up our leading positions in the firm; on the contrary, we considered the further conduct of the business as our principal assignment in life. We expected to preserve our inheritance and all the responsibility connected with it, if at all possible, even beyond our generation. We would not have founded SSW corporation in such a way that would have made it impossible to preserve our top management positions."

9. According to the annual report of AEG for 1902/03, in 1902 Siemens, AEG, and the Felton & Guilleaume Group combined held a share of three-quarters of Germany's electrotechnical production.

10. In answer to a committee conducting a survey, Carl Friedrich von Siemens attributed Schuckert's difficulties above all to its engagement in the electrochemical industry; yet its considerable engagement in the contractor business might well have had an even more important influence. See "Verhandlungen," pp. 409ff.

11. See SAA 69/Lr 515; 11/Le 862; "Fünfzig Jahre AEG," pp. 149ff. Also see notes by Felix Deutsch in the Leo Baeck Institute, New York.

12. In 1901–2 there were long-drawn-out negotiations between AEG and Schuckert over establishing an association with common interests, possibly later resulting in a merger. The banks represented in the Schuckert syndicate pursued this course owing to the unfavorable financial development of the company. In 1902 the negotiations were considered to have failed and were discontinued. On January 14, 1903, Roland Lücke, a board member of the Deutsche Bank and member of the supervisory board of Siemens & Halske, started confidential preliminary talks with the privy councillor A. von Rieppel, a

member of the supervisory board of Schuckert who had also conducted the negotiations with AEG. At another conference on the same day, Wilhelm von Siemens declared that his firm was in no real need of such a merger, but that the activities of AEG would make it advisable. According to a report by von Rieppel, the merger with AEG would have taken place had the financing business of Schuckert and the great volume of stock of the financing company Continental Company for Electrical Endeavors (Continentale Gesellschaft für Elektrische Unternehmungen) not deterred AEG and caused it to withdraw. See SAA 28/Li 987.

13. See SAA 4/Lf 682; 722; Riesser, *Großbanken,* pp. 544ff.; Feldenkirchen, "Finanzierung," pp. 101ff. A marginal note by the director of the Deutsche Bank, Carl Klönne, jotted down on a letter from Dr. O. von Petri, the director of SSW, April 24, 1912, may provide a clearer picture of the conditions resulting in the founding of SSW: "If Petri sees the SSW's main source of income, soon after its founding, in Nuremberg, this would be a strange perception. In any case, the improvement in the Nuremberg results was caused by the energetic initiative of the Berlin management, the appropriate transfer of certain production lines to Nuremberg, shifting the production of other items to Berlin, in short, by the totally new organization.—It should not be forgotten that Schuckert was almost bankrupt when Rieppel approached Lücke for help."

14. BA Potsdam, Assets 80, Ba 2, Deutsche Bank No. 18850.

15. See Czada, *Elektroindustrie,* p. 50.

16. A letter written by Wilhelm von Siemens to the lawyer Koechlin-Hoffmann in Basel, February 28, 1914, reads:

> Please avoid using the phrase Siemens-Schuckert Concern.
> The term concern connotes something indefinite, nothing that
> is pleasant. Our company and the Schuckert Company, at any
> rate, do not make up a concern as expressed in common us-
> age. We are two companies operating completely indepen-
> dently of one another. They are united neither by common
> capital nor by any associations in the management. Also, the
> activities of the two companies are generally different. Our
> company is purely industrial, whereas the Schuckert Com-
> pany operates mostly as a contractor. The common denomi-
> nator of the [two] different [establishments] Siemens and
> Schuckert in Germany consists in the fact that both are part-
> ners in a private limited company. For us this part in the part-

nership does not have the character of a portfolio investment, as, for example, a bank would classify such a form in its books, but it is a part, a most important one at that, of the comprehensive industrial enterprise. We have, in order to preserve this structure, at the occasion of the founding of SSW, expressly reserved for ourselves the right to keep the legal seat in Berlin and the majority share of the partnership, and also on the supervisory board, in that S & H has the statutory right to appoint the chairman, and his vote also secures the majority. . . . We consider it most important not to have the matter presented as if S & H had split their enterprise into different companies and the common link were to be made up only of different partnerships. On the contrary, the centralized management of the centralized enterprise has been cultivated to an even greater extent than had been the case before. We chose this way only because we did not want to create too great a number of new S & H stockholders. (SAA 54/Ll 618)

17. SAA 69/Lr 515.

18. The legal structure of a private limited company, chosen at the founding of SSW, was not based on concerns over taxation, even though the obligation for limited companies to pay income tax had only been introduced in Prussia in 1906. As Siemens & Halske and Schuckert had committed themselves to conduct their entire business in the field of electric power from the company's own capital, creating new stock and offering the shares to the public to finance the new company would have constituted an increase in number of shares, and thus a dilution of the stock of the company. If no shares were offered, the status of a public corporation made no sense for the time being. See Findeisen, *Unternehmensform,* p. 128; Brandstetter, "Finanzierungsmethoden," p. 63.

19. SAA 37/Lp 872.

20. For the policy concerning the annual balance, see also SAA 20/La 246.

21. For information on the financing of enterprises, see Feldenkirchen, "Finanzierung," and also "Zwischenkriegszeit." For the development of the workforce and for sales figures of Siemens & Halske and SSW in the period of time between 1903/04 and 1913/14, refer to the tables in the appendix.

Bibliography

Photos were taken from the Siemens Archives.
The graphs are based on data in the tables in the appendix.

Archives

AEG Archives, Frankfurt am Main
Archives Deutsche Bank, Frankfurt am Main
Archives Siemens AG (SAA), Munich
Bundesarchiv (BA), Potsdam
Leo Baeck Institute, New York

Literature

Borchardt, Knut. *Die industrielle Revolution in Deutschland.* Munich, 1977.
————. "Wirtschaftliches Wachstum und Wechsellagen, 1800–1914." In *Handbuch der deutschen Wirtschafts- und Socialgeschichte,* edited by W. Zorn, vol. 2, pp. 198–275. Stuttgart, 1976.
Brandstetter, Erich. "Finanzierungsmethoden in der deutschen elektrotechnischen Industrie." Diss., Gießen, 1930.
Chandler, Alfred D. *Scale and Scope: The Dynamics of Industrial Capitalism.* Cambridge and London, 1990.
Cohen, Rudolf. *Schuckert, 1873–1923.* Würzburg, 1923.

Conrad, Christoph. *Erfolgsbeteiligung und Vermögensbildung der Arbeitnehmer bei Siemens (1847–1945)*. Beiheft 36 der *Zeitschrift für Unternehmensgeschichte*. Wiesbaden, 1986.

Czada, Peter. *Die Berliner Elektroindustrie in der Weimarer Zeit*. Einzelveröffentlichungen der Historischen Kommission zu Berlin, 4. Berlin, 1969.

Dettmar, Georg. *Die Entwicklung der Starkstromtechnik in Deutschland*. Vol. 1. Berlin, 1940.

Dynamik und Dimensionen der deutschen Elektroindustrie. Special publication of *Elektrotechnik*. Frankfurt am Main, n.d.

Ehrenberg, Richard. *Die Unternehmungen der Brüder Siemens*. Vol. 1: *Bis zum Jahre 1870*. Jena, 1906.

Eibert, Georg. *Unternehmenspolitik Nürnberger Maschinenbauer, 1835–1914*. Beiträge zur Wirtschaftsgeschichte, 3. Stuttgart, 1979.

Elektrotechnische Zeitschrift, 1880.

Fasolt, Friedrich. "Die sieben größten deutschen Elektrizitätsgesellschaften. Ihre Entwicklung und Unternehmertätigkeit. Eine volkswirtschaftliche Studie. Nebst einem Anhang: Die zahlenmäßige Entwicklung der deutschen elektrotechnischen Industrie, ihre örtliche Verteilung und ihre Gliederung." Phil. diss., Heidelberg, Borna-Leipzig, 1904. Also: Mitteilungen der Gesellschaft für Wirtschaftliche Ausbildung e.V., Frankfurt am Main, vol. 2. Dresden, 1904.

Feldenkirchen, Wilfried. "The Export Organization of the German Economy." In *Business History of General Trading Companies: The International Conference on Business History, 13: Proceedings of the Fuji Conference*, edited by S. Yonekawa and H. Yoshihara, pp. 295–331. Tokyo, 1987.

———. "Die Finanzierung der deutschen Elektroindustrie in der Zwischenkriegszeit." In *Zur Geschichte der Unternehmensfinanzierung*, edited by Dietmar Petzinap, pp. 35–68. Schriften des Vereins für Socialpolitik NF, 196. Berlin, 1990.

———. "Zur Finanzierung von Großunternehmen in der chemischen und elektrotechnischen Industrie Deutschlands vor dem Ersten Weltkrieg." In *Beiträge zur quantitativen vergleichenden Unternehmensgeschichte*, edited by R. Tilly, pp. 94–125. Historisch-Sozialwissenschaftliche Forschungen, 19. Stuttgart, 1985.

Findeisen, Franz. *Unternehmensform als Rentabilitätsfaktor.* Berlin, 1924.

"Fünfzig Jahre AEG." Manuscript. n.p., n.d.

Goetzeler, Herbert, and Lothar Schoen. *Wilhelm und Carl Friedrich von Siemens: Die zweite Unternehmergeneration.* Stuttgart and Wiesbaden, 1986.

Heintzenberg, Friedrich. "Carl Heinrich von Siemens: Ein Lebensbild nach seinen Briefen." Unpublished manuscript, Siemens Archives.

Helfferich, Karl. *Georg von Siemens.* 3 vols. Berlin, 1921–23.

Henniger, Gerd. "Elektrifizierung in Preußen: Ein Beitrag zur Geschichte der Elektrifizierung der Industrie, 1890–1914." Diss., East Berlin, 1988.

Henning, Friedrich–Wilhelm. *Die Industrialisierung in Deutschland, 1800–1914.* 7th ed. Paderborn, 1989.

Hertner, Peter. "German Multinational Enterprises before 1914: Some Case Studies." In *Multinationals: Theory and History,* edited by Peter Hertner and Geoffrey Jones. Aldershot, 1986.

Hoffman, Walther G. *Das Wachstum der deutschen Wirtschaft seit der Mitte des 19. Jahrhunderts.* Berlin, Heidelberg, and New York, 1965.

Kaelble, Hartmut. *Berliner Unternehmer während der frühen Industrialisierung: Herkunft, sozialer Status und politischer Einfluß.* Veröffentlichungen der Historischen Kommission zu Berlin, 40. Berlin and New York, 1972.

Keuth, Heinz. *Sigmund Schuckert: Ein Pionier der Elektrotechnik.* Erlangen, 1988.

Kieve, Jeffrey. *The Electric Telegraph: A Social and Economic History.* Newton Abbot, 1973.

Kirchner, Walther. *Die deutsche Industrie und die Industrialisierung Rußlands, 1815–1914.* St. Katharinen, 1986.

Kocka, Jürgen. *Die Angestellten in der deutschen Geschichte, 1850–1980: Vom Privatbeamten zum angestellten Arbeitnehmer.* Göttingen, 1981.

———. "Siemens und der aufhaltsame Aufstieg der AEG." *Tradition* 17 (1972): 125–42.

———. *Unternehmensverwaltung und Angestelltenschaft am Beispiel Siemens, 1847–1914: Zum Verhältnis von Kapitalismus und Bürokratie in der deutschen Industrialisierung.* Industrielle Welt, 11. Stuttgart, 1969.

———. *Unternehmer in der deutschen Industrialisierung.* Göttingen, 1975.

Loewe, Joseph. "Die elektrotechnische Industrie." In *Die Störungen im deutschen Wirtschaftsleben während der Jahre 1900 ff.*, vol. 3.3. Schriften des Vereins für Socialpolitik, 107. Leipzig, 1903.

Matschoß, Conrad. *Werner Siemens: Ein kurzgefaßtes Lebensbild nebst einer Auswahl seiner Briefe.* 2 vols. Berlin, 1916.

Michel, Andreé, and Frans Longin. *Siemens: Trajèctoire d'une entreprise mondiale.* Paris, 1990.

Peschke, Hans-Peter. *Elektroindustrie und Staatsverwaltung am Beispiel Siemens, 1847–1914.* Europäische Hochschulschriften, 154. Frankfurt and Bern, 1981.

Pohl, Hans. *Aufbruch der Weltwirtschaft: Geschichte der Weltwirtschaft von der Mitte des 19. Jahrhunderts bis zum Ersten Weltkrieg.* Stuttgart, 1989.

———. "Zur Geschichte von Organisation und Leitung deutscher Großunternehmen seit dem 19. Jahrhundert." *Zeitschrift für Unternehmensgeschichte* 26 (1981): 143–78.

Pohl, Manfred. *Emil Rathenau und die AEG.* Berlin and Frankfurt, 1988.

Pole, William. *Wilhelm Siemens.* (German edition of the *Life of Sir William Siemens,* 1888.) Berlin, 1890.

Remy. *Die Elektrisierung der Berliner Stadt, Ring- und Vorortbahnen als Wirtschaftsproblem.* Berlin, 1931.

Riesser, Jacob. *Die deutschen Großbanken und ihre Konzentration im Zusammenhang mit der Entwicklung der Gesamtwirtschaft in Deutschland.* 3rd ed., rev. and enl. Jena, 1910.

Sawall, Edmund. "Die Unternehmenskonzentration in der Elektroindustrie: Stand, Motive und Organisationsformen." Diss., Karlsruhe, 1963.

Schumpeter, Joseph Alois. *Business Cycles: A Theoretical, Historical and Statistical Analysis of the Capitalist Process.* New York, 1939.

Siemens, Georg. *Der Weg der Elektrotechnik: Geschichte des Hauses Siemens.* 2 vols. 2nd ed. Munich, 1961.

Siemens, Werner von. *Lebenserinnerungen.* 18th ed. Munich, 1986.

———. *Wissenschaftliche Abhandlungen und Vorträge.* 2nd ed. Berlin, 1889.

Tilly, Richard. "Verkehrs- und Nachrichtenwesen, Handel, Geld-, Kredit- und Versicherungswesen, 1850–1914." In *Handbuch der deutschen Wirtschafts- und Sozialgeschichte,* edited by W. Zorn, vol. 2, pp. 563–96. Stuttgart, 1976.

Trendelenburg, Ferdinand. *Aus der Geschichte der Forschung im Hause Siemens*. Technikgeschichte in Einzeldarstellungen, 31. Düsseldorf, 1975.

"Verhandlungen und Berichte des Unterausschusses für allgemeine Wirtschaftsstruktur (Enquete–Ausschuß). I. Unterausschuß 3. Arbeitsgruppe 1. Teil: Wandlungen in den Rechtsformen der Einzelunternehmungen und Konzerne." Berlin, 1928.

Wagenführ, Rolf. *Die Bedeutung des Außenmarktes für die deutsche Industriewirtschaft*. Sonderheft des Instituts für Konjunkturforschung, 41. Berlin, 1936.

Waller, Ernst. *Studien zur Finanzgeschichte des Hauses Siemens*. 5 vols. Bound manuscript. (= SAA 20/Ld 366.)

Weiher, Sigfrid von. "Carl von Siemens, ein deutscher Unternehmer in Rußland und England." *Tradition*, 1956, 13–25.

———. *Die englischen Siemens-Werke und das Siemens-Überseegeschäft in der zweiten Hälfte des 19. Jahrhunderts*. Schriften zur Wirtschafts- und Sozialgeschichte, 38. Berlin, 1990.

———. *Werner von Siemens: Ein Leben für Wissenschaft, Technik und Wirtschaft*. Göttingen, 1966.

Weiher, Sigfrid von, and Herbert Goetzeler. *Weg und Wirken der Siemens-Werke im Fortschritt der Elektrotechnik, 1847–1980*. 3rd ed. Berlin and Munich, 1981.

Wessel, Horst A. *Die Entwicklung des rheinischen Nachrichtenwesens in Deutschland und die rheinische Industrie*. Beiheft 25 der *Zeitschrift für Unternehmensgeschichte*. Wiesbaden, 1983.

Winterfeld, Ludwig von. "Entwicklung und Tätigkeit der Firma Siemens & Halske in den Jahren 1847–1897." Diss., Berlin and Naumburg, 1913.

Historical Perspectives on Business Enterprise Series
Mansel G. Blackford and K. Austin Kerr, Editors

The scope of the series includes scholarly interest in the history of the firm, the history of government-business relations, and the relationships between business and culture, both in the United States and abroad, as well as in comparative perspective.

American Public Finance and Financial Services, 1700–1815
Edwin J. Perkins

The Passenger Train in the Motor Age
California's Rail and Bus Industries, 1910–1941
Gregory Lee Thompson

Rebuilding Cleveland
The Cleveland Foundation and Its Evolving Urban Strategy
Diana Tittle

Daniel Willard and Progressive Management on the Baltimore & Ohio
Railroad
David M. Vrooman